SNIPPETS
OF A
CHRISTIAN

HUMOR, HOPE &
ENCOURAGEMENT

Nana

Sue Desautels

outskirtspress

DENVER, COLORADO

Snippets of a Christian Nana
Humor, Hope and Encouragement

Cover design by Travis Schrock. Author photo by Anthony Heyward, Sr. All rights reserved - used with permission.

Biblical References:

Scripture quotations taken from the New American Standard Bible, Copyright 1960, 1962, 1963, 1968, 1971, 1972, 1973, 1975, 1977, 1995 by the Lockman Foundation. Used by permission.

Scripture quotations taken from the Amplified Bible, Copyright 1954, 1958, 1962, 1964, 1965, 1987 by The Lockman Foundation. Used by permission.

KJV – King James Version, Public Domain – No copyright information available

NKJV: Scripture taken from the New King James Version. Copyright 1982 by Thomas Nelson, Inc. Used by permission. All rights reserved.

Scripture quotations marked (NIV) are taken from the Holy Bible, New International Version. NIV. Copyright 1973, 1978, 1984, 2011 by Biblica, Inc. Used by permission of Zondervan. All rights reserved worldwide. wwwzondervan.com The "NIV" and "New International Version" are trademarks registered in the United States Patent and Trademark Office by Biblica, Inc.

Scripture quotations marked (ESV) are from The Holy Bible, English Standard Version. (ESV), copyright 2001 by Crossway, a publishing ministry of Good News Publishers. Used by permission. All rights reserved.

Outskirts Press, Inc.
http://www.outskirtspress.com

ISBN: 978-1-4787-0006-7

Outskirts Press and the "OP" logo are trademarks belonging to Outskirts Press, Inc.

PRINTED IN THE UNITED STATES OF AMERICA

DEDICATED TO THOSE IN SEARCH OF HOPE,
NEEDING A WORD OF ENCOURAGEMENT, AND
LONG FOR THE SOUND OF LAUGHTER

Table of Contents

Prologue

Snippets of a Christian Nana – A collection of short stories and daily postings of encouragement and hope. Many of these stories are glimpses of my life as a young Christian, military wife, and mother. Some are humorous, some are reflective, and some are unexplainable. I believe God has allowed some uncomfortable and embarrassing moments to come into my life to open my eyes to the messier side of life. I learned to be humble. I learned that I don't need kids to embarrass me; I do quite well on my own. I learned not to take myself so seriously. I have attached a scripture to each short story. I love how the Bible has a scripture for even the funnier side of life. Some may be a stretch with the story but the scripture stands alone. You can apply it to your life, your situation, and your peace of mind.

Hopefully, my stories will put a smile on your face. My desire for you is to realize you can get through any challenge that comes your way by having hope, laughter and the Word of God in your life. Each journey is unique to the individual and each one of us has the potential for greatness.

ENCOURAGEMENT

What an amazing word! It searches the soul to inspire to a greater sense of purpose and meaning in a world filled with much hurt and heartache. To be inspired and to have laughter is the beginning to understanding the blessings of God's goodness in our lives.

Introduction

The times of my life – I was born in the 1950's, became an Air Force brat in the 1960's, and settled in central Massachusetts in the 1970's. I still carry the New England accent with me. My story is a glimpse inside a young military family, finding laughter in times of tense situations, and experiencing hope in the worst. I have learned that God has been with me in the best of times and He has lifted me up during the worst. I met my husband, Ron, when I was fifteen, engaged at sixteen, and married at eighteen. We had four children: Jessica (Jessy Bessy), Jason (Jay Bay), Joshua (Josh b Gosh), and Jennifer (Jenni Benni) by the time I was twenty-five. My children make me laugh, inspire me, challenge me, and make me very proud. They have their own stories to share, so I will not, but I hope they know I adore them and that God has a great plan for each of their lives.

I have five grandchildren to date: Jacob, Jaslyn, Vincent, Andrew, and Lorelai. They are the great joys of my life. We have been doubly blessed in having bonus grandchildren, Brian and Amanda. Who knew one of my greatest loves would be through my grandchildren. I find it almost impossible to discipline them in any way, and in my eyes, they can do no wrong. I don't know when that happened, and I certainly wasn't that way with their parents, but there is something almost beyond reproach when it comes to them. Each one has such a unique way of bringing me such inspiration and laughter. I love their honesty, their questions, and their unconditional love for everybody.

My mother has made her home with us since 1996 and she has blessed our lives richly. Her spirit is always positive, uplifting, and encouraging. She also has the New England bluntness to tell it like it is. She has a forgiving heart and she works in our yard every single day, making it the envy of the entire neighborhood.

I gave my heart to Jesus in my teens, I backslid in my forties, only to be redeemed in my fifties. I am a work in progress. I am certainly not perfect. Yet God wakes me each morning to begin anew. God has surrounded me with angels on earth, my extended family. I have a core of golden friends who share my spirit and I love them dearly.

We may be a little dysfunctional, but I have heard that dysfunctional is now the new functional family. All families are unique, beautiful, and weird. My husband retired from the Air Force and we now live in one of the most beautiful areas in the Country, Charleston, South Carolina. We are blessed to have flowers all year round. Ron is not only my husband, but he is truly my best friend. He makes me laugh every day, and we can read each other's minds, which scares my husband beyond belief. As my mother says, "we are what we are." I am so grateful for all the moments of my life, and for God's amazing grace.

CHAPTER ONE

Embarrassment Never Takes A Vacation

Coming face to face with yourself

After ten years of marriage and four kids, we finally had scraped up enough money to go on a honeymoon. After giving our friends a long list of phone numbers, stocking the refrigerator full of food, and some tears from our youngest we were finally on the road - Free at last to do what we want, when we wanted to do it! We checked in to our beautiful hotel room, at the Comfort Inn, and the first thing I did was check out the television shows (did I mention we had been married ten years). A new movie was coming on called *Salem's Lot*. How exciting, we could actually watch a grown up television show and the best part was David Soul, *Starsky and Hutch* fame, was the leading man. Yes, life was good.

Now Ron is a wonderful provider, husband, father, friend, and eternal optimist. Ron's favorite part of staying in a hotel was playing the game, "look for the money". Ron always believes there is a bag of money just waiting for us to pick up and spend, we just have to look for it and look he did. I tried to explain to him that if there had been any money to be found that the maid service would have already found it. He was not deterred by my negative talk, and he would be the one to find it. As long as he was quiet and I could watch my "grown-up" TV show - we were all winners. This may be a good time to let you know that I am terrified of horror movies. I can't even watch a commercial about a scary show without having nightmares…so imagine my surprise as *Salem's Lot*, about vampires, started to unfold – scary!

Now you can see my dilemma, turn the channel or keep watching David Soul. I was determined to be an adult, to be brave and watch David Soul to the very end. The scarier the show got, the more the sheets came up around me. I could see Ron out of the corner of my eye still searching for his treasures. Now he is getting on his hands and knees to look under the bed, the absolute best place to hide money.

Just as the dead began to rise up, just as my heart was racing, just as the sheets were up to my eyes ready to cover my head in just a few seconds, suddenly Ron let out a scream of horror. It was a scream so deep you knew it was real, a scream so horrifying that I just knew that Ron had found something, a body, a dead body decaying under our bed. As Ron screamed, so did I. Ron held on to the bottom of the bed with his knuckles white and his face washed of any color. I held on to the sheets, screaming in unison, now knowing that we would die in a horrible vampire type way. I finally yelled out, "RON, WHAT IS IT?"

As he composed himself, breathing heavy and throwing his upper torso on to the bed, he simply said, "mirror". That is right, when he looked under the bed he saw himself. Apparently, because people would lose their valuables under the bed, the hotel had placed a strip of wood covered in a glass mirror around the bed frame, hence keeping anyone from losing anything valuable! Death by mirror finding – truly scary!

SCRIPTURE:

He will yet fill your mouth with laughter and your lips with shouts of joy. Job 8:21 (NIV)

WORDS OF ENCOURAGEMENT FOR THE WEEK:

DAY ONE – Are you cursed or are you blessed? Are you Pooh Bear or are you Eeyore? Are you claiming the best or are you doomed to fail? Do you aim for the light or is darkness ever present? Lord, I will choose to name my blessings, I will see the world through the eyes of a child, I am claiming victory, before I know the end. I will do my best knowing you are in control. I am walking in the light because you are with me always.

DAY TWO – A cup of faith from us is like a cup of espresso to God. An appetizer of obedience from us is like bacon-wrapped scallops to God. A plate mounded with trust, worship and praise from us is like a Thanksgiving feast to God. A bowl of humbleness from us is like a warm homemade apple pie to God. What are you feeding God today?

DAY THREE – Our minds were never meant to carry the burden of stress and worry. It is like an infectious disease that will spread throughout your body and could in fact kill you. Has it ever helped? Does it resolve anything? Is it satisfying in any way? So why do we do it? Like many of you, I have had a tough week. It is hard to watch a loved one going through a trial or illness. Today is a new beginning. I may not be able to fix the difficulties of life but I know someone who can. Forgive me Lord for forgetting who you are. Having peace in my heart is the best medicine I have taken all week.

DAY FOUR – Someone told me yesterday that never in a million years would they believe I would grow my own vegetables, learn to sew, or write a book. He said, "Has the whole world gone crazy?" "What planet am I living on?" "Am I living in another dimension?" "Alright", I said, "I get it, I have changed." Today I challenge you to do something unexpected. People see you one way, but God sees you another way. You have been made with a purpose. Let God transform your life in such a way that even your closet friends will not recognize you!

DAY FIVE – Imagine yourself sailing out on the water when suddenly a storm catches you by surprise. The waves are so high that the boat capsizes and you fall out. You see a life buoy close by and you swim over to it and hold on for dear life. The waves are crashing against your body and just when you think you're not going to make it, a hand reaches down to pull you up. The voice says, "You must let go of the buoy you're holding on to", but you don't want to let go of the buoy. The buoy has kept you afloat during the storm, BUT the hand promises to take you out of the storm and bring you safely to dry land to a future. I am prayerfully asking you to let go of the buoy and trust God to pull you up. I know it's scary, I've been there myself, but the best thing I have ever done was to let go of the buoy and take His hand.

DAY SIX – "Sleep well knowing that God never does!" Author Unknown

DAY SEVEN – May this day bring you satisfaction, determination, dedication, examination, gratification, illumination, affection, protection, and revelation. What a day of celebration!

Visiting the "Bates" motel

The travel brochure described our two star hotel as being family oriented with a large pool, two bedroom suites, playground for the kiddies, and even vibrating beds. Sounded like heaven in a nut shell, for a young military family moving to North Dakota. We had never been to Canada so we took this opportunity to just relax after driving all day.

As we pulled up to the hotel, I started to get a sinking feeling that this wasn't "family" oriented. When we checked in, I noticed that the man at the front desk looked a little bit like *Beetlejuice* with a cigar. On the way by, we passed the pool that had no water but did have a green slime that looked like something from a Chernobyl meltdown and I swear I saw something moving slowly underneath the green slime. We opened the door to our "suite" where there were three double beds and I was thinking none of them would have passed the black light inspection.

Being the eternal optimists that we are, we asked the kids if they wanted to lie on a vibrating bed. I mean really, how cool would that be? As luck would have it, they did, so I dug out fifty cents per bed and watched them shake. Well, after about thirty seconds they wanted it to stop. I have to confess, it wasn't as much fun as I thought it was going to be. We told them it would stop soon and they should be grateful that they were able to experience a vibrating bed, not all kids in the world had that luxury. We went onto our side of the room to unpack when, all of a sudden, the kids started yelling. We ran in to see the beds shaking quite hard now and Jason was screaming as he could not feel anything from the waist down. I yelled at Ron to unplug the beds, so he scrambled to find the plug. The problem was it didn't shut them off. Now I have to tell you, I was really starting to get creeped out by this time.

We grabbed the kids and went out to supper. As Ron went in to tell manager about the beds, we walked past the playground. I happened to notice that there was a popped balloon on the ground. Josh ran over to pick it up when I realized it was not a balloon. I yelled, "STOP" at the top of my lungs. I hurried the children into the minivan and off we went to eat. Since Jenni was having some issues with asthma and feeling grumpy we went back to the motel. We told ourselves that these kinds of things happen and we will just make the best of it. I decided that we would just go to bed and get some rest. Unfortunately, resting wasn't going to be in our immediate plans that evening. We got back, put the kids to bed, and just collapsed ourselves. All of a sudden Jenni started screaming and breathing heavy, sounding like Darth Vader. I brought her into the bathroom and turned on the shower to full hot steam.

That's when she started describing "dinosaurs" that sounded a lot like demons coming at us. Now Jenni wasn't yet three and she seemed horrified, giving us many details of each beast. Ron and I began to pray and each time Jenni would announce that the "dinosaurs" had gone away. After a few hours of continually praying and Jenni freaking out with each new beast, we made the decision to throw our clothes in our suitcases, grab the kids and get the heck out of dodge. That's as close as we ever came to an Alfred Hitchcock motel, and I still shiver when I think about it.

SCRIPTURE:

"I sought the Lord, and He answered me, and delivered me from all my fears." Psalm 34:4 (KJV)

WORDS OF ENCOURAGEMENT FOR THE WEEK:

DAY EIGHT – The Voice of Faith
For evil whispers in my ear,
the silence means He does not hear.
All hope is lost,
the end is near,
but now my faith will make it clear.
He has not moved away from me
for in His time I soon will see.
I feel His strength,
I hear His call,
I know He reigns above us all.
Report the news I do know now,
I trust and keep His holy vow.
I chose to praise His holy name,
for in His glory,
He remains the same.
He was, He is, He will come again,
for now I know to carry on
to complete the task at hand.
For soon enough He'll call me home
and I will reap the eternal throne.

DAY NINE – Release the positive power of your words, speak them out loud. There is strength on the tongue and your voice will break through the negative forces around you and your loved ones. The positive word is like a force field around you and your loved ones, protecting against the darkness. A negative word is also like a force field, not letting any goodness into your life and heart.

DAY TEN – For a designated moment in time, your destiny has been anointed. Last year, last month, even last week would have been too soon, but now you are hearing the call. You are casting off the rags of worry and fear. You have been given the royal robes by God Himself. Rise, stand, and be counted, for your appointed hour has come.

DAY ELEVEN – The choice has always been yours. You have been chosen, so that you will listen to the call and then choose wisely.

DAY TWELVE – Do you have spiritual bad breath? Do you gossip? Are your words full of bitterness? Do you complain about everyone and everything in your life? Are you mean-spirited, fault finding, judgmental, cruel and negative? Don't panic, you just have to gargle with the scripture once a day, unless you're spiritually ill, in that case every four to six hours as needed. Don't forget to attend your local Bible believing church, and for your spiritual cleansing, floss with encouragement, praise, worship, kindness, humbleness, gentleness, truth, courage, and inspiration. I am sure very soon you'll have that beautiful, spiritual, sweet smelling breath once again.

DAY THIRTEEN – Sweet is the sound of silence – it stirs my soul to listen for His voice. I praise Him while I wait and reflect on what needs to be done. As with each moment that passes, I catch a glimpse of the day beginning to stir. The quiet, the stillness, the gentle approach, my day begins now for I hear His voice calling my name.

DAY FOURTEEN – What is the difference between superstition and faith? Superstition has to be acted upon believing if you do or don't do something that your prayers will be answered. Faith is giving all your cares, all your problems, and all your heartache to God. You can do nothing in your own right – it's all God, His timing, His deliverance, and His power. Yes, we pray, than we let God do what He does best. Now step back and let Him show you how faith works.

Eating outside our comfort zone

The year was 1988 and Ron was on a one year remote assignment with the USAF. He was able to come home at the half way point and we decided to take the kids out of school for a few days and head to Cape Cod. October was such a beautiful time of the year to go to the Cape. Now up to this point our main eating out consisted of McDonald's and Pizza Hut, but Ron wanted to take his beloved young family to a nice "grown-up" restaurant. Looking back I see now there were many clues that suggested that we should stop the crazy talk about eating out at a nice place, but we threw caution to the wind and went anyway.

First clue, there were many cars in the parking lot, such as, BMW's, Cadillac's, and Lexus'. Then there we were, pulling up in our minivan, a little dirty, some wear and tear, all managing to stumble out. I tried the best I could to comb cowlicks down, and re-tuck in shirts. Second clue, as soon as we walked in you could tell this was way out of our league. I looked at Ron and said, "Do you want to leave?" At this point our nine year old son, Jason, started to panic. Jason was a great little guy but he was a very nervous kid. He was horrified to think we might leave a restaurant before even being seated. Jason started tugging on my sleeve and urging us not to leave that everyone would be looking at us. I assured him that no one was staring at us and to keep moving (but seriously, everyone was looking at us). Clue three, the hostess wasn't rude but she gave us a look like the "Beverly Hillbillies" had just walked in. As we passed the tables, I noticed there was no one under the age of 65 and many of the men were smoking pipes (a sign of class and sophistication) and ladies were in their Boston best. The seats were high winged, living room chairs and the tables were elegant in their crisp, white linens with polished silver and sparkling crystal. Many of the patrons had thick books in hand discussing literary classics, I'm sure. There were fireplaces around to keep everyone cozy and warm. The closer I got to our table the more I knew we had made a terrible mistake. Clue four, the children's menu started at $10.95 for the beef stroganoff, which made me physically ill.

Now, the rest of the evening was more like a blur, but I'll give you the highlights. My water glass spilled two times, by the way cloth napkins really do not absorb, but my white cotton pants did manage to absorb most of the water. Our youngest fell asleep while waiting for her food to come out. So, Ron and I were eating our food, but eating Jenni's too. My third child, Josh, who was seven years old at the time, tried shoveling in too much at once and began gagging, and just in case no one was watching us, my son Jason, the nervous one, started yelling, "Mom, Josh is throwing up on the table". "MOM, Mommy, Mom, MOM, Mom, Mommy, MOM" well, you get the idea. The bill came to $126.00 and we ended up with a bad case of indigestion. Even after all these years we still manage to feel slightly uncomfortable in a grown up restaurant setting.

SCRIPTURE:

"If any of you lacks wisdom, you should ask God, who gives generously to all without finding fault, and it will be given to you." James 1:5 (NIV).

WORDS OF ENCOURAGEMENT FOR THE WEEK:

DAY FIFTEEN – I awoke in the middle of the night to the sense-less chatter of my mind. In the darkest hour I was unsure what was expected of me. I am vulnerable to the elements of my worst fears. I quiet my spirit from the uninvited voices that explode in my mind. I will not take this path again. I will bring my mind under the authority of the Holy Spirit. I may have begun in con-fusion, but I don't have to stay there. These are the times that God speaks with clarity and I hear Him best of all. I will focus on the praise. I will remember His promises and I will relinquish my control over to Him.

DAY SIXTEEN – Grateful
Grateful for the rising sun
Grateful for the risen Son.
Grateful I can get around
Grateful I can hear the sound.
Grateful for my family and friends
Grateful to the very end.
Grateful I can stay at home
Grateful for the Masters Throne!

DAY SEVENTEEN – It is normal to be upset or hurt when someone is mistreating us. The problem comes when we absorb the hurt, when we collect the words into our mind, and when we drink in the poison of hate, anger, and bitterness. We are giving the enemy all the power. You are better than that! You are not what your enemy says you are. Release yourself from this torture. Our God has a great plan for your life, but you won't be able to see it because your eyes are too filled with the hurt, the pain, and the heartache. Let today be the day you stop carrying your enemy on your shoulder. I believe in you, you are a precious gift to this world, and more importantly God believes in you. Push through - I know you can do it!

DAY EIGHTEEN – I am the model Christian…when I am home alone. I am wise, compassionate, and patient…when I am home alone. I am generous, sensitive, and dare I say share Agape love… when I am home alone. The issue seems to get murky when I actually have to leave the house. We can't hide away forever. Open the door and step outside. God doesn't expect us to be perfect in every way. He does expect us to try, to call out to Him, and to love everyone!

DAY NINETEEN – It's not about the problem – it's about the trust. It's not about the blame – it's about the truth. It's not about the illness – it's about the journey. It's not about the hurt feelings – it's about the forgiveness. I was doing it all wrong until I gave it to God. When I gave it to Him and left it with Him, I received peace and joy in my heart.

DAY TWENTY – I don't have to know the how's, the why's, the who's, the when's and the where's. I just know He will, He does, He can, He knows, and He is!

DAY TWENTY-ONE – When the answer to your prayers are "no", He is either protecting you or preparing you for the greater good. Nothing is random with God.

Who cares what you look like

I thought we would never get out of Virginia traveling with four generations of Desautels', who were irritable and exhausted. We had been traveling all day and what normally took four to five hours became twelve hours due to summer bumper to bumper traffic. Instead of trying to get home to Charleston, South Carolina, we all decided to spend the night as soon as we crossed the North Carolina border. We decided to go eat out and just relax; as I passed the mirror I have to confess I looked a mess. My hair, which is short, was sticking up and over to the side, due to napping in the car. I appeared to have laid my head against the window exposing half my face towards the sun, which was now sunburned, while the other side was still whiter than white. I can't honestly remember if I had even brushed my teeth (now, now, no judging). I was wearing my favorite jogging outfit, which I never jogged in, but was so comfortable for traveling. I noticed that my two year old grandchild had been pulling on my shirt and it had stretched out exposing some of my under garments. I debated whether or not to just hop in the shower and change my clothes, but I got a lot of resistance from the family, who were just as tired and very hungry.

My mother's comment to me was, "who cares what you look like, who even knows you're here, we are four hundred and fifty miles away from home, let's just go and eat." That made sense to me, so out we went. We decided to go to a Western Sizzler type place. I just tried not to make eye contact since I looked, well, pretty awful. I had the satisfaction of knowing that everyone in our group all looked about the same, so who cares, we're away from home. The hostess began to seat us when all of a sudden a man yells from across the restaurant, "Ron, is that you?" "Oh my goodness is that Ron Desautels, from church?" "What are the odds?" "It's a small world, isn't it?" I was thinking the same thing, seriously, what are the odds?

As Ron went over to talk with them, my mother leaned in and asked me if I wanted to fix my hair..."No", I said, "No?", my mother repeated, "No", I said again, they can see me in my full glory. Of course they were dressed like they had just left church. At times like those I have to ask myself, why can't we ever run into somebody who looks, well, like us? I like to think when these kinds of things happen it is God's gentle way of keeping us humble.

SCRIPTURE:

"Rejoice in the Lord always; again I will say, Rejoice." Philippians 4:4 (KJV)

WORDS OF ENCOURAGEMENT FOR THE WEEK:

DAY TWENTY-TWO – No matter the day...I'm His. No matter the ending...I'm His. No matter the decision...I'm His. No matter the outcome...I'm His. It is a great feeling to know that He is in control and I can finally let it go.

DAY TWENTY-THREE – Don't let your negative mouth dictate your positive day!

DAY TWENTY-FOUR – Stop trying to interfere with a situation that still needs to play itself out. Remember in the Old Testament when Sarah was just trying to help God? Sarah complicated an issue that should have never happened. You can also complicate a promise by trying to "help" God. Let God be God. If He wants to bring you in to the plan, He will call you. By Tania Burgbacher

DAY TWENTY-FIVE – While watching a sporting event, at the Special Olympics, I was inspired with how truly happy all the athletes were. As they ran around the track each one was giving 100% to cross the finish line. The one in last place looked just as happy as the one in first place. Many of these young boys and girls had to overcome incredible hardships to even make it that far. My question had to be – Why can't we, who have been given so much, be happy? Stop looking at your limitations and stop complaining. Be encouraged to finish the race, cross over joyful, inspired, and strong.

DAY TWENTY-SIX – Well meaning bad advice is still bad advice – listen to God's voice, He always has the best advice for YOUR life.

DAY TWENTY-SEVEN – Just because you can talk doesn't mean you should.

DAY TWENTY-EIGHT – While cleaning out my closet to make room for the next season, I was reminded that I should also clean out my spiritual closet. Putting away my worldly thinking, taking out fear, stress, anxiety, bitterness and replacing everything with the belt of truth, the breastplate of righteousness, the shield of faith, the helmet of salvation and the sword of the spirit.

DAY TWENTY-NINE – I am expecting a miracle today. I am accepting God's grace and mercy. I will have a positive effect by showing kindness and compassion today. I will accept that I cannot do it alone. Let me affect my neighbors in a positive way.

DAY THIRTY: Are you feeding the light with your positive words, your kindness, your forgiveness, and your love or are you feeding the dark with fear, with bitterness, and stress? Make no mistake you are feeding one of them. One will grow and prosper, while the other one will wither and die! Listen to what you're saying!

DAY THIRTY-ONE: God's specialty is fixing the broken.

CHAPTER TWO

CLASSIC DESAUTELS'

You're invited to a birthday party

While we were visiting up in Massachusetts, my little cousin invited us to his wife's birthday party. They live in New Hampshire but we had a GPS to get us there. So off we go, Ron, me, and my mom. It took about an hour and a half, but as we started turning down the side roads we noticed there were a lot more twists and turns, and it was getting hilly. The GPS said turn now, but I thought I saw out of the corner of my eye there was a different street name. Ron started calling off the numbers to the houses, and suddenly there it was, 364, and they were nice enough to put balloons on the mailbox.

As I looked out the window, I didn't recognize one single person. I said to my mother, do you recognize anyone? My husband spoke up first and said, "Well, Patrick is on the fire department, so they are probably his friends". I was still uneasy, even though we hadn't lived up north in years. I should be able to recognize at least one person. My mother spoke up next saying, "look at those kids, they are as Irish as they come, of course they're our people". Still not 100%, we get out and start to mingle. Everyone was so nice, and brought us over to the buffet to get something to eat and drink. Just then an older lady came walking up to us and said, "Can I help you?" I said, "Yes, we're here for Jennifer's birthday party". Smiling and looking around the room. Then she said,

"What street are you looking for?" Then I knew, the little Irish kids were not our people, the young adults were probably not friends of my little cousin, and heaven help us, we just crashed someone else's party (by the way, it was graduation weekend up north, so everybody seemed to have balloons on their mailboxes). Upon telling them the street address, one young man said, "It's two streets up".

We started apologizing and backing up to the car, as the entire party seemed to follow us out. I let my mother in first, just in case it got ugly, then I turned to the entire graduation party and said, "if for some reason my cousins party is boring we'll be back," with that everyone started laughing and wished us well. They said come back anytime. You have got to love those New England yankees.

SCRIPTURE:

> "Keep on asking, and you will receive what you ask for. Keep on seeking, and you will find. Keep on knocking, and the door will be opened to you." Matthew 7:7 (AMP)

WORDS OF ENCOURAGEMENT FOR THE WEEK:

DAY THIRTY- TWO – Three powerful words you can say that can change someone's life forever - I forgive you!

DAY THIRTY-THREE – Did I leave the conversation with encouragement? Did I end the meeting with hope? Did I send my kids off with prayer? Did I remember to thank God? Did I speak, think, and act in a way that is pleasing to Him?

DAY THIRTY-FOUR – God is the great recycler – He will turn your trash into treasure. He will piece together the broken. He will shine the dull. He will find a new use for the outdated. He will restore, re-program, re-plant, separate, reclaim, convert, redeem, regenerate, rescue, restore, salvage, and take back for His glory!

DAY THIRTY-FIVE – Can't sleep? Maybe it's the only time He can get your attention. It is a great time to pray and share your heart with God.

DAY THIRTY-SIX – Fear will rob you of relationships, sleep, joy, and physical health. Fear will paralyze your life. Fear will eat you from the inside out. Have you ever played the "what if" game? Stop it; that game has fear written all over it!

DAY THIRTY-SEVEN – My prescription for you today is laughter! You can giggle. You can smile. You can throw your head back and explode with a hardy laugh. Laughter will bring strangers together and keep you young. Giggling will tickle the soul and dissolve the stresses of the day. Hysterical laughter from others will bring a smile to your face. Laughter will heal the heart like no other medicine. It will carry out all the toxins inside of your body. The great thing about laughter is that there are no side effects. Today, make it a point to laugh like no one is watching.

DAY THIRTY-EIGHT – The many miracles of God: immediate – every day – walk through - in time – by and by – instant – process – multiplied – magnified – glorified – redeemed. All wisdom, all grace, all mercy comes from God and it is all a miracle – take God out of the box and know it is in His perfect timing to bring the greatest glory to Him.

Going on vacation with friends

The thing about going on vacation with friends is that sometimes you might do things you might not normally do, go places you might not normally go, and say things you might not normally say. This reminds me about the time we went on a cruise with seven other couples from church. There were four out of the seven couples enjoying the pool side, playing ping pong, sleeping, or in my case reading my new kindle, every once in a while looking up to watch the children play on the water slide. Suddenly I heard Ron squeal as he sailed down the water slide. I had to smile at his carefree attitude to enjoy every moment, no matter how silly he may have looked. One of my friends commented that Ron seemed to be really enjoying himself and at that moment a thought crossed my mind. I was going to have some fun myself. After all, what was I waiting for? Sometimes I don't know what gets in to me.

I looked at my friend, Deb, and said to her, "let's do it, let's go down the slide". Now the one thing I love about Deb is that she is always up for a good time. I said, "Let's not let life pass us by, let's grab the gusto and appreciate each minute", and she replied, "let's do it!" So up the stairs we headed, with each step I started to realize we were going up pretty high. I guess by my face Deb could tell I was having second thoughts, and said, "we only live once, let's do this". Now Ron gave me some great advice about going down, he said, "lay down, and fold your arms across your chest," he assured me he would be waiting at the bottom to help me up.

Sitting at the top of the slide was quite overwhelming, but there was the church group, chanting us on to just do it…so I said, "Let's do this!" I was pumped, I laid down, crossed my arms and down I went. Now what I didn't know was that Deb was still at the top. What I didn't know was by lying down and crossing my arms over my chest I would go faster. What I didn't know was that the speed can sometimes shift clothing around. So you could hear me screaming all the way down until the bottom, where it drops and I went completely under. What I didn't know was that I would be totally submerged and with my mouth open I got a mouthful of water. Panic set in and I was threshing and coughing as I made it to the surface.

At that point I realized that some of my clothing might have "moved," and the first person I saw was my beloved husband Ron, taking pictures like the paparazzi and praising my performance. The next thing I remember is the life guard at the top of the slide telling my friend she had to go down and yelling for me to move. There were kids waiting! Oh my goodness, could I really get up without knowing if everything was in "place"? What could I do with everyone watching? I went right into a panic prayer, Lord, cover me up, Amen. Is that a vain prayer? I'm going to say, no. I think I can speak for the entire church group when I say; it was a prayer worth praying. As far as I know everything was secure, and it was something else I could check off my bucket list!

SCRIPTURE:

So I commend the enjoyment of life, because nothing is better for a man under the sun than to eat and drink and be glad. Then joy will accompany him in his work all the days of the life God has given him under the sun. Ecclesiastes 8:15 (NIV)

WORDS OF ENCOURAGEMENT FOR THE WEEK:

DAY THIRTY-NINE – If we practiced our Faith as much as we give in to our fear, we would be mighty indeed.

DAY FORTY – Having joy in your heart during the midst of the storm doesn't mean you're in denial, it just means you gave it to God and left it with Him.

DAY FORTY-ONE – I remember the hurt, but it will not rob me of my joy. I remember the past, but I will not live there anymore. I remember the struggles, but it doesn't hold me down. I remember the pain, but it will not stop me from serving those around me. Lord, let me use my hurt, my past, my struggles, and my pain, so that I may be a blessing to others in the future.

DAY FORTY-TWO – On this particular cruise we decided to splurge and get a large cabin window in our room. We loved being able to open the curtains as soon as we woke up to see the vastness of the ocean and breathtaking sunrises each morning. On the second day, we had just come into port. While we were finishing up breakfast, we decided to just skip going into Freeport altogether and just lounge by the pool. Ron was in the bathroom and I was trying to hurry up and change in the cabin. We wanted to get a good chair nearest the pool. Suddenly I heard the horn of a tugboat. I looked up to see the tugboat drifting by with the crew all smiles and waving as they passed by my open window. I learned a very important lesson that morning. Only leave your curtains open while you are actually out to sea. I don't think we give enough credit to those beautifully private interior rooms that we will again chose on our next voyage out to sea.

DAY FORTY-THREE – The failures we experience in our life are nothing more than lessons we needed to learn to get to our final destination.

DAY FORTY-FOUR – Your unforgiveness and bitterness go hand in hand. Choose something better for yourself. You deserve it! Nothing says "in your face" better than living a happy and forgiving life!

DAY FORTY-FIVE – Are you expecting a miracle today? Is something great about to happen? Wake up every day with expectations – begin the day with hope, with purpose, and with a mission to complete. I'm excited to see how the day unfolds. I will look for the things that will inspire me today. I will be encouraged simply because I woke up and know He has given me another chance.

Weighing in on a question that begs to be asked

There are some things that we just know without having to be told and sometimes we just have to go out and find the evidence and hold the proof in our own hands. How much does the human head weigh? Depending on where you go to look up the answer, it can be anywhere from eight to twenty-one pounds. So, you can see why I felt the need to begin my own research. No? Well, the scientist inside me beckoned me to start my own research. No? Ok, I was just curious, a stay at home mom, all the kids were in school - take your pick.

We need to travel back to the early 1990's. We lived in Illinois, stationed at Scott Air Force Base. I had always suspected I had a heavy head, not a fat head, not a *Charlie Brown* head, but a heavy head none the less. I remember one night while watching TV in our bedroom, and my head was resting on Ron's chest. The more relaxed I became the more I let my head relax, and then I noticed Ron's breathing seem to get labored, like it was getting more difficult for him to take a deep breath. As I lifted my head, his breathing became easier. I also noticed I had to always sleep with two or three pillows, and in the morning they were flat as a pancake. You're probably saying to yourself, wow, her head does sound heavy.

I decided to ask some dear friends of mine, non judgmental friends, friends who were brilliant and supportive. The ones I knew would have the answers I sought to my personal and potentially embarrassing question. How much does the human head weigh? After much laughing and friends bringing other friends over to laugh, I was told it was not possible to know how much the human head weighs. I held my head high as I told them I would make it my mission to find out, something inside me said, "they're laughing now, but soon, very soon, they'll all be sorry." Ok, I may have over reacted a bit, but I would have my answer. The next day I pulled out the bathroom scale and placed it on the living room floor.

Fortunately for me I have four kids, and I was able to enlist the weight of their heads too. Six, seven, nine, and ten, all respectable head weights, we wrote our research down. There was a neighbor boy who had come over and was watching, he also wanted to weigh his head. I would have loved the extra research, but it hit me that this may be some form of child abuse.

I told him he could as long as he asked his mom first and he never came back. Now it was my turn. I laid there waiting for the numbers to spin up, when my husband came home from work. He saw me lying on the floor with all our children around me. Ron walked over, bent down, and said, "What time is supper?" I said it would be on the table in a few minutes, I was just weighing my head. Ron never questioned my unorthodox methods, he just accepted me where I was and I have always loved that about him.

At the next church fellowship I had some scientific knowledge to share with my brothers and sisters in Christ. My head weighed in at twenty-three pounds, thank you very much! They never let me live it down. At least God loves me, right?

SCRIPTURE:

"A cheerful heart is good medicine, but a crushed spirit dries up the bones." Proverbs 17:22 (NIV)

WORDS OF ENCOURAGEMENT FOR THE WEEK:

DAY FORTY-SIX – How many ripples will your stone touch as it skims across the lake? Our spirits also make a ripple that skims across the lives we meet. Who will be touched as you skim by? What will the effect be? As we are the master to the rocks we throw, our Lord is the Master to our lives. He will direct the aim to make the most exquisite designs across the tapestry of our lives.

DAY FORTY-SEVEN – God could call you at any moment to change the world. Make sure He has your number!

DAY FORTY-EIGHT – <u>Nana moment:</u> I stand amazed how two strangers can enter my life and come through the front door straight into my heart, becoming a part of our family forever. I love to be able to see them with the same eyes and love of a Nana's heart. This love is truly a gift from God – love you Brian and Amanda!

DAY FORTY-NINE – The Blessing
There is a presence that surrounds me
and a joy that fills my heart.
What a blessing to receive God's favor
from the very start.
I will not disappoint Him
I have a journey to complete.
One day I hope to bring a crown
to lay across His feet.
What a glorious day He has given
and a blessing to behold.
I work each day knowing
that He is in control.
No matter how I'm feeling,
no matter what they say
My hope rests in knowing
He is my King all day today!

DAY FIFTY – March can be a remarkable month to keep in mind all the miracles around you. Don't hold malice in your heart or get mad when life gets messy. You can be the model of a magnificent human being. Today is not a day to be mundane but to unlock the mysteries of your mind. Learn to mix it up a bit. Break the mold of what you think Mondays should be – You are mighty, you matter, change your mind set. The letter M was brought to you today by our motivated Master.

DAY FIFTY-ONE – What does the day hold for you? Are you going to work? Are you driving in some crazy traffic? Are you getting the kids ready for school? What is your normal? Is your normal not normal? Did the alarm clock forget to go off? Did you get a flat tire going into work? Are the kids sick again? Whether everything runs smoothly for you or everything seems to go wrong. You need to stay the course. Be strong, be brave, be courageous, be still, and know that He is God!

DAY FIFTY-TWO – The less you have, the better God can work through you.

The Grand Opening

The one thing I love about grand openings is that they are so GRAND! Everything is over the top. The store really goes the extra mile to show off each department. Ron and I entered the sparkling new store, Ron said, "I'll meet you in one hour". I checked my watch, nodded my head, and turned right, while Ron turned left. I have to admit the store went the extra mile, having school mascots, every aisle had samples of yummy treats, and each end cap had a place to fill out your name and number for a drawing. I hadn't even gotten to the Ladies apparel when all of a sudden I see Ron, walking briskly towards me. Oh for goodness sake, I thought, he said one hour. Before I even had a chance to say anything, Ron comes right up to me, taking my arm and says, "Let's go." I said, "Let's go?" "Yes," he said again, "Let's go!" "Why?" I said. "I haven't even gotten to the free hors d'oeuvres yet". He comes in closer, whispering in my ear, "I'll tell you when we get outside". "No, I want you to tell me now," I could tell by his demeanor he really wanted to leave NOW. My next thought (which I'm not proud of) was did he steal something? I have a very active imagination, so I wasn't going anywhere until he confessed his "sin".

Ron looked around, lowering his head, he began to confess all. He said he was walking around eating the samples, enjoying all the displays and mascots. When Ron entered the tool department he walked straight over to the items on sale.

He suddenly noticed a young man dressed in full costume. Ron was very impressed with how well this young man had gone all out for the tool section. He was stiff like a robot, and he wore metal screws, even a rod up his back, with a halo around his head. Ron was so impressed he started clapping and said, "Job well done, robot man." Ron was imitating the robot moves of the young man. Unfortunately, the young man was not amused and he said some things to Ron that would have made any sailor blush. He had been in a car accident and he was in traction. Traction vs. Mascot can be hard to tell the difference sometimes. Ron obviously confused him with the "tool man" mascot. A natural mistake in my opinion, so needless to say, we left immediately.

SCRIPTURE:

"for if you forgive men their trespasses, your heavenly Father will also forgive you." Matthew 6:14 (NKJV)

DAY FIFTY-THREE – If you believe all your troubles stem from your ex, your spouse, your kids, your work, your church, your siblings, your parents, your teachers, your neighbors, your pastor/priest...come closer; it's not them, it's YOU! Let it go, seriously, let it go, or you are going to be a very lonely person.

DAY FIFTY-FOUR – Release your grip on a problem that was never meant for you to handle.

DAY FIFTY-FIVE – Does anyone else know the couple Mr. and Mrs. Crank E. Hanks? I'm sure you know them. They are the beautifully dressed couple that always seems to show up when you have made a mistake. They will address your mistakes immediately and probably in front of a group. They believe their gift in life is to inform the rest of us what we are doing wrong. They raised their children correctly, they have their doctorates in all subjects, they can preach the best sermons, and they know all the answers – hey, wait a minute, no they don't. I'm telling you don't listen to them. They are angry, prideful people. Good news for you...God accepts you right where you are. He will encourage you and lift you up. Next time that happens to you, look up, not around!

DAY FIFTY-SIX – Sometimes it seems like I have spent most of my life waiting. I was waiting for the answered prayer, waiting for test results, waiting to start, waiting to finish. I waited for the kids to leave home only to then wait for them to visit us. Do you ever feel like "the waiting" is sucking the life out of you? I used to think that waiting was a waste of time until I slowly began to realize waiting was actually a hidden gift in disguise. Next time you find yourself waiting, slow down the pace and see what God wants you to see. Start by serving others while you wait, develop your character. These are the times that hope, faith and dare I say patience will begin to take shape. Nothing is a waste of time with God. Waiting is a valuable tool. Waiting is a plateau in helping you reach your fullest potential.

DAY FIFTY-SEVEN – Sweet is the day that wakes you up and you realize you have been given another chance.

DAY FIFTY-EIGHT – Where would I be without the struggles? I have learned to appreciate, to admire, to grow, to be humble; to realize there comes a time and a season for all things.

DAY FIFTY-NINE – It's not about the understanding but about the believing. It's not the end but a new beginning. It's not the silence but listening for the voice. It's not being fearful but controlling the thoughts. It's not the negative energy but choosing the joy in spite of the challenge. It's not the failures but learning valuable lessons. It's not about the heartbreak but about the breakthrough.

CHAPTER THREE

THE EVERY DAY MIRACLES OF GOD

"I Helping Mommy"

The year was 1979. I was the mother of a two year old little girl and a newborn baby boy. Our baby boy was born a month early and I believe he was trying to catch up by eating every hour on the hour. Jason would let out a wail for his next bottle right at the one hour mark, just as regular as the clock. His older sister, Jessy, hated to hear her precious little brother crying. She would always tell me to "hurry mommy, Jason needs you". As Jason began to work up quite a bellowing cry, I went right into the kitchen to warm up his bottle.

Just as I was testing the milk on my arm to make sure it was the right temperature, I suddenly realized Jason had stopped crying. I immediately went into the hallway to see, much to my horror, my two year old holding my newborn son in her arms. Trying not to panic, I quickly scooped Jason in my arms and checked to make sure he was okay. As I took him out of her arms, Jessy said proudly, "I helping mommy".

A wave of relief came over me when I realized he was fine and quite hungry. I bent down and gave Jessy a hug and gently told her that only mommy or daddy could get Jason out of the crib. Looking into Jessy' little cherub face, I could see she was so proud that she could help me. I gave Jason his bottle and he drifted off to sleep for an hour. I brought him into his nursery which was filled with *Winnie the Pooh* decorations and gently placed him back in to his crib.

I stopped dead in my tracks when I saw the potential horror of the scene played out in front of me. I saw the chair pushed up against the crib. Jessy reaching in to pick up her newborn baby brother and somehow jumped off the chair while holding Jason in her arms. She then held him going down the hall to bring him to me. You cannot convince me there is no such thing as angels.

SCRIPTURE:

> "For He will command His angels concerning you to guard you in all your ways; they will lift you up in their hands, so that you will not strike your foot against a stone." Psalm 91: 11-12 (NIV)

WORDS OF ENCOURAGEMENT FOR THE WEEK:

DAY SIXTY – While visiting my daughter in Syracuse, we noticed the cutest and the tiniest baby skunk walking around their yard. I didn't think it was a good idea to go outside and get up close and personal, but the girls assured us that new born skunks don't spray. So why not go for the gusto? We all ventured into the yard. I have to say the baby skunk was so adorable, so little, and so sweet. Until he turned around, balanced on his front little legs, and lifted his tail. I was amazed how fast four intelligent adults went running, screaming, and pushing through the sliding-glass door like the boogeyman was after us. Fact: Even if the books say one thing, when you're faced with either being logical or facing a potential stink bomb, you put all logic aside and run like you're on fire.

DAY SIXTY-ONE – During my time of self reflection I must ask myself – What am I showing the world? What is my legacy? What will people miss most about me when I am gone? Lord, may I be humble in my actions. I pray I bring encouragement to those around me. Let me bring laughter to a hurting world. These are all noble actions, but Lord, may your light in me shine bright above all these.

DAY SIXTY-TWO – "Do you love me?" The voice was becoming more frequent now. My response, "Lord, you know I love you" – I was confused. I heard "do you love me" when I woke up, when I went to bed, and whenever my mind began to drift. I believe the Holy Spirit was speaking straight to my heart – He was telling me that I could no longer be comfortable doing what I had always done. I was no longer a baby, or a child, or even a teenager. I had to walk out in faith, become a spiritual adult, to totally trust Him. As my relationship with God evolves, the less I hear do you love me, but when I do, I know it's time to change once again into the person I need to be. Do you love Him?

DAY SIXTY-THREE – Each season is meant to inspire, to humble, to renew, to open your eyes, to rebuild, to transform, and to deepen your relationship with Christ.

DAY SIXTY-FOUR – Do not let your past mistakes steer you into a dead end of misery. Learn from those mistakes to be a catalyst for your future success. What you do today; could very well have an impact on your family tomorrow.

DAY SIXTY-FIVE – "Be still my child", His voice says to me, "Do not listen to the confusion that surrounds you." "Do not turn to the left or to the right." "Stay the course." "My plans for you are mighty". In my morning devotional today, I believe God spoke this to my heart, for my spirit needed to hear His voice.

DAY SIXTY-SIX – Am I in the plan? How come I don't see any results of my labor? Why is it so hard? I am so tired and it is so messy, why me? I am here to tell you that you are in the plan. Life is messy and you will get dirty. You have a destiny to fulfill. Do not let the negative people of this world distract you. Don't let the pain turn you bitter, you are one of a kind my friend.

The love of a brother

The first game of the Miracle League baseball fall season was about to begin and there was excitement in the air. Everyone was getting a chance to bat and run the bases. There are two innings where everyone gets to play and everyone gets to feel the excitement of running/riding into home plate.

The other team was up first. I remember thinking as the first boy came to bat, what was his disability? He didn't need any help getting to the base or hitting the ball into left field, first pitch. As he began to run to first base, he turned to his right and grabbed the wheel chair that his sister was sitting in and took off running. The crowd cheered this brother and sister team on. The little boy was running so fast, that between second and third the wheelchair went up on one wheel. The crowd came to its feet, hoping in some way to help this pair from falling over. You could hear the gasps in the bleachers.

The little brother, managed to get the wheelchair back down and with a full steam of speed he ran to home base. As they crossed the home plate, I could see his sister's disabilities were many, but she had the biggest grin on her face. It was a priceless moment for all that got to witness this great sporting event, on that early Saturday morning in the park.

SCRIPTURE:

"Even small children are known by their actions, so is their conduct really pure and upright." Proverbs 20:11 (NIV)

WORDS OF ENCOURAGEMENT FOR THE WEEK:

DAY SIXTY-SEVEN – Have you ever imagined what God looks like? I can see Him sitting on His throne, so massive are His majestic robes that they cascade down and overflow onto the floor stretching out beyond the edges of heaven itself and still the robes continue to flow. Cherub angels flying around His very throne, praising and lifting up the name, the Great I AM. I can also picture Him kneeling gently by my bed, holding my hand, while I am consumed with sorrow and hurt. Whispering in my ear He loves me. Whether you picture God as the King of kings or as our heavenly Father, He loves you and wants only the best for you. He will protect you, comfort you, and inspire you. He will challenge and stretch you. Go to Him now, for He longs to hear from you personally.

DAY SIXTY-EIGHT – I know it's not easy to love someone who is cruel to you, or to forgive your enemies, especially after an abusive episode. This commandment may very well be the hardest thing you ever do in this life. Hear me friends, if you want God's blessings, if you want to move to the next level, if you want peace of mind, you MUST forgive and you must expose kindness into the face of cruelty. So, hold on, be strong, and know that you will reap what you sow – and so will they.

DAY SIXTY-NINE – Don't you see, the spiritual test is our reaction. No matter if someone cuts us off while driving down the highway or the waitress who ignores us completely. No matter how someone treats us or how someone else is driving is not the point. How we react is what God is watching. We cannot respond to a situation that has nothing to do with us. We are accountable for our own actions. Let them pass by. Smile when faced with indifference, you may make a difference today in their lives and lower your blood pressure tomorrow.

DAY SEVENTY – When will the change happen for me? God will use me when I begin to release my fear to Him. God will bless me when I stop my constant complaining. God will give me wisdom when I start to trust and acknowledge Him in all ways. God will give me peace when I take my hands off the problem, when I realize it has never been about me, but always about Him.

DAY SEVENTY-ONE – One prayer
One prayer ushers in the angels,
one prayer sweeps away the pain.
One prayer cuts to pieces evil,
one prayer transforms our very brain.
One prayer builds a force field round us
one prayer shields us from the storm.
One prayer brings us transformation,
one prayer bring our dreams to form.

One prayer shows His tender mercies,
one prayer lets us know we're loved.
One prayer sends our God a message,
one prayer brings the holy Dove.

DAY SEVENTY-TWO – When you receive the negative report. When all the experts tell you what can't be done. When all seems hopeless, do not meditate on the negative; for God has the final word. Speak only the positive, pray out the impossible; believe in His power. Let the journey be the testimony you share tomorrow.

DAY SEVENTY-THREE – Every person born was made for a purpose, a destiny, and is part of the missing puzzle piece to His plan! There are no mistakes with God.

Super stars in the most unusual places

My very first Special Olympics caught me off guard with the organized chaos and wonderful volunteers who had come out to support the kids. The excitement of all the children and other schools was a joy to watch, but what really touched my heart and had me digging through my purse for a tissue was the young man who sang the national anthem. As the young man came to the podium, he went right up to the microphone and started to sing, but they weren't quite ready. So, the gentleman who was with him covered his mouth.

They raised the American flag and everyone put their hand over their hearts. Then, the man removed his hand from this young man's mouth. Within thirty seconds I needed a tissue. He was not a good singer. His notes were all off key, but he knew every word. It's hard to put into words how dedicated this young man was to sing this song. This was a great honor for him and I couldn't help but believe that God was standing next to this young man, beaming with pride. His facial expressions and body language were perfectly in tune with the song. For he was making the most beautiful noise of all, he was singing from his heart, with all the passion he had within him. I tell you my friend, no singing artist today could even come close to his singing abilities.

SCRIPTURE:

> "Rather let it be the hidden person of the heart, with the incorruptible beauty of a gentle and quiet spirit, which is very precious in the sight of God." 1 Peter 3: 4 (NKJV)

WORDS OF ENCOURAGEMENT FOR THE WEEK:

DAY SEVENTY-FOUR – The enemy may seem like they are winning for a season, but don't be fooled by the physical – God is watching and His word is final.

DAY SEVENTY-FIVE – I used to let others take care of all my spiritual growth. I let the Pastor read the Bible for me. When I needed prayer, I would ask my Christian friends to pray for me because their prayers were so elegant and perfectly stated. I assumed if I raised my children in church and we tried living a Godly life, everything would just fall in to place. I was living in "La La land". Imagine my surprise when the problems came and

I didn't know how to defend myself against the spiritual enemy. In God's mercy and grace, He is transforming me. The Bible is my sword and my comfort. I speak to God directly in all matters. Begin today and watch God's power transform your life.

DAY SEVENTY-SIX – There will be days when it seems hopeless, but I choose to praise Him. There will be days when I wonder if He hears my prayers, but I know He does. There will be days when those around me will question my decisions, but I say God is in control. He knows my heart and He knows my name…I choose to Praise!

DAY SEVENTY-SEVEN – When the challenges of life seem overwhelming, remember, this is when God does His best work. To show us He changed the hearts. He healed the body. He cast out the vengeful spirits. He saves, He comforts, He heals, He changes; He is forever and always.

DAY SEVENTY-EIGHT – How will you survive? Only God can put the pieces of your heart together again and let it begin beating once more.

DAY SEVENTY-NINE – Indifference, sitting on the fence, expecting the worst, and constant complaining will open the front door to the devil allowing him to come in and literary destroy your life. The best decision I ever made was to change my mind set and to close the door to the enemy. I will focus on the blessings, the joy, and the love of Christ in my life.

DAY EIGHTY – Are you waiting? Are you praying?
Are you anxious? Are you trusting?
Are you nervous? Are you praising?

Are you scared? Are you believing?
God has an answer for all situations, pray, trust, praise and believe!

I Held a Miracle today

The prayers were ten years in the asking
In the late summer of their lives
When all the doctors had reported
It would not be possible to thrive.
Who could have foreseen this tragic loss?
Only God and time knew best.
Never hearing a heartbeat of the other three,
it was all still such a great tragedy.
The decision was made for them you see,
their time had passed them by,
and now we grieved along side of them,
wondering what was to be.

All the shots, the hormones, the daily charts
to close this chapter was the hardest part.
Now, what we did not comprehend,
was that God's hand was still over them.
It never left you see,
for what man says is impossible,
God speaks life into thee.
He saw their struggles, He felt their pain,

He heard their cries at night.
He knew this small child of theirs
would be destined for the light.

Celeste and Scott knew their time had come.
Don't ask them how they knew,
for God had placed this in their hearts,
and they knew what they had to do.
The doctors agreed more testing must be done at once,
but no, the answer came.
What God has given us this day,
was simply meant to stay.
I held a miracle today.
Her name is Olivia.
She is perfect in every way.
A beauty to behold,
made by the Master's hand to serve,
to love, and to hold.

SCRIPTURE:

"Do not be anxious about anything, but in every situation, by prayer and petition, with thanksgiving, present your requests to God. And the peace of God, which transcends all understanding, will guard your hearts and your minds in Christ Jesus." Philippians 4:6-7 (NIV)

WORDS OF ENCOURAGEMENT FOR THE WEEK:

DAY EIGHTY-ONE – Nana moment: At age four, Jacob rested his head on my arm. He looked tenderly up at me and said, "I love your arms Nana, they are just like pillows," then he squeezed his arms around me. Best compliment ever! Only a grandchild could say this and make my heart melt.

DAY EIGHTY-TWO – As much as I hate the word goodbye, I treasure the memories we made today. Until we meet again, may God be ever at your side. May He direct your path; throughout your journey. May I carry a piece of your spirit in my heart, letting others see you shining through. May you remember our time together with laughter and love.

DAY EIGHTY-THREE – As a Country, I thought we had evolved further in our society than how our prime time television portrays us. We watch the very rich vs. the very poor, the north vs. the south, and finding true love in a matter of weeks. Even these people aren't living a "real" life, we are still stereotyping people. Look at people the way God sees them. He spent much time making each one unique and special.

DAY EIGHTY-FOUR – God knows it's been difficult for you, but you will not find peace in the quick remedies of drugs and alcohol. God is putting into your life avenues to get the help you need. You are not alone. He is with you every step of the way. He wants you to be well. He wants you to be whole and He wants you to experience the joy you deserve. Let today be the starting point, no matter how many times you've tried. You can begin fresh today. You are worth it, you are loved, you are one of a kind, and God has a great plan for your life.

DAY EIGHTY-FIVE – I cannot control how people think. I cannot control the actions of others. I cannot control malice, gossip, hate, or envy. Knowing this sets me free from worry, stress, anxiety, and turmoil. I can control my own thoughts. I can control my own actions. I can control my own tongue. I can give it to God.

DAY EIGHTY-SIX – It's only natural to be upset when you're going through a struggle or challenge, but don't let the negativity of the situation dominate your mouth. You can talk about the negative, but do it in a positive way. Does that make sense? Instead of talking endlessly about the problem try saying God is in control. He has a plan. I do not have to know the details. Simply trust that God will take care of you.

DAY EIGHTY-SEVEN – We are climbing to the top of the mountain but falling less. When the giants stand in front of us we run through their legs. When we are told it cannot be done we show them how it is working. We will not accept the struggles but embrace the possibilities. We will not listen to the negative but focus on the victories. Today is your day – make it the best day possible!

CHAPTER FOUR

AWKWARD MOMENTS

Not speaking with our "inside" voices

Remembering to talk with your inside voice has been somewhat of a challenge for our family, and by inside I mean not sharing every thought that comes into our mind out loud. One time in particular, we were at the church for our quarterly Sunday school meeting. We sat at round tables of eight. There were all ages represented at our table and it was just nice to be able to fellowship and discuss the topics for the next quarter. As we were winding down with our meeting, one elderly lady at our table mentioned that she needed to go out west for a few weeks. Ron asked her if she was going to be visiting relatives and her response was, yes, she going to visit her mother.

That's when everything started to slow down. When you've been married as long as we have, you can actually read the other persons mind and I did not like what I was hearing. "You're MOTHER?" Ron said in a rather loud voice. Now in all fairness to Ron, the lady was in her seventies, but still. Ron continued on, "Dear lord, your mother is still alive?" How many times do I wish I could have taken that sentence back for him? Alas, that was not meant to be on that particular Tuesday evening. On a side note, isn't it amazing how one sentence can stop all other conversation around the table?

I then went into some damage control, and quite frankly I didn't do a very good job, but I had to try. I blurted out, "Isn't it wonderful your mother is still alive, Ron's mom passed away a few years ago" (hoping for the sympathy angle). There was a moment of silence. Then the lady raised one eyebrow up, looking at Ron she said, "Yes it is." On the way home, Ron and I discussed once again about using our inside and outside voices.

SCRIPTURE:

"Whoever guards his mouth and tongue keeps his soul from troubles." Proverbs 21:23 (NKJV)

WORDS OF ENCOURAGEMENT FOR THE WEEK:

DAY EIGHTY-EIGHT – Sometimes being backed into a corner gives you a better perspective to see when God enters the room.

DAY EIGHTY-NINE – One evening, while working at the store, some thoughts crossed my mind. "You have no spiritual gifts". "God can't use you." "You have been away from Him too long." I had recently just started going to church after a long absence. Just for a moment I agreed with the thoughts that came in to my mind. Then I put them aside and continued working. About an hour later my Life Group leader came into the store. She had never been there before, but she believed God was telling her to come to the store to encourage me. She wanted to share with me what God had laid on her heart about my spiritual gifts. I only had the thought for a moment or two, yet God responded immediately and wanted me to know I am very important for His kingdom. I am here to tell you the same thing. You, my friend, are very important, you do matter. God does care greatly about every part of your life. God uses people every day to share the good news.

DAY NINETY – God wants you to expose your scars. They show you were in the battle and survived. When you look in the mirror you can remember in all humbleness where you came from. A great example of a man who shares his scars is Dave Roever. If you have time check out his testimony at http://roverfoundation.org.

DAY NINETY-ONE – I am claiming victory today as I stand alone in the storm. I am claiming victory today as my knees buckle beneath me. I am claiming victory today as the pain is almost too difficult to bear. I am claiming victory today because I know He has a plan. Father, give me your hand for I cannot do this alone. Give me courage to face this day. Quiet my spirit to wait on Your timing.

DAY NINETY-TWO – When tempers start to flare, the strongest person in the room is usually the one who remains quiet and prays.

DAY NINETY-THREE – I find the more I give to Him, the more peace He gives to me.

DAY NINETY-FOUR – How long you are in a season depends a lot on your mindset. Take back the control of your mind. Don't fill it up each morning with fear, worry, and doubt. There will be no room for joy, breakthroughs or peace. Let today be your turning point…stop seeing yourself as the victim. You are the chosen! You have been made with a purpose, a goal and a destiny. Set aside this day for the renewing of your mind and watch how God can transform your life.

Making a good first impression

Serving on the new members committee is very rewarding and right up my alley in what I love to do. I love encouraging new members and new Christians, helping them find their place in ministry. One evening a young couple came through the class, Dr. Tron and his beautiful wife Erica. I was instantly taken by them. They were outgoing and had great smiles. I went up during a break to introduce myself to this hip, young couple. Now, I hate to brag, but I do pride myself on being able to talk to almost anybody about almost anything. I asked them where they were originally from. Dr. Tron said he was from the Poconos and Erica was a Jersey girl. Well, well, well, my northern neighbors, I am originally from Massachusetts so I knew we were going to be the best of friends.

I told them that Ron and I had been to the Poconos for our tenth wedding anniversary and that we had a great time. Then it happened, Dr. Tron said, "that is great, what kind of activities did you do there?" That's when the unimaginable happened – my mind went blank, I could not think of one activity we did. The longer the pause, the more uncomfortable we all became. Erica was nodding her head up and down, finally trying to give me some options. Did you go ice skating? How about skiing down the beautiful mountainside? Horseback riding was awesome in the winter season. Did you go down any of the trails? With each question I shook my head, no, but my mind was racing, say something you idiot. Make something up these are not brain surgery questions – TALK! Nope, nothing, I could not seem to remember one thing we did.

Finally Dr. Tron said smiling, "So, you didn't do anything?" "We did", I blurted out, "we were on our second honeymoon so you know, well we pretty much just stayed in our room." I don't know who was more shocked, me or them. There was enough embarrassment on everyone's faces. Erica and Dr. Tron gave out a nervous laugh, which I'm sure just what they wanted to hear from a middle aged nana. I ended up saying a few more things and then I abruptly turned and moved along. I was mortified. Why couldn't I just say a simple white lie? I told my husband Ron that I hope I never see those two anytime soon. The awkwardness would be too much to bear.

But God has a sense of humor and He knows when certain spirits are meant to be together. We ended up becoming dear friends with them and we even hosted a life group together in their home for a while. I love them to life and we still chuckle at that embarrassing moment when we first met. I could have missed out on a great story if I had told a white lie, and by the way, there is no such thing as a white lie.

SCRIPTURE:

"Fulfill ye my joy; that ye be like minded, having the same love, being of one accord, of one mind." Philippians 2:2 (KJV)

WORDS OF ENCOURAGEMENT FOR THE WEEK:

DAY NINETY–FIVE – Even if it's hard, press forward. Even if you're afraid, still believe. Even when you're tired, take your stand. Even if you don't know how to pray, call out to Him. Even when you can't see any results, praise His holy name.

DAY NINETY-SIX – No matter the kind of day I am having, I know from experience, that I am better with Him than without Him.

DAY NINETY-SEVEN – Are you still comparing yourself to others? Now why would you, the hero in the story, do that? Everyone else is just a team player, but not you. You are the one to lead, to stand out, and to carry the message to the masses. You are certainly not ordinary. Now, put your sunglasses on, roll down the window, and soar.

DAY NINETY-EIGHT – As I was walking out of the restaurant the other night, a very pretty and stylish woman was coming in. I noticed out of the corner of my eye that she did a double take when she saw me. So I looked back at her. She was smiling broadly, so I smiled back at her. She said, "You look great," I said the same to her. She said, "It had been ages." I agreed. We hugged and said good-bye. I wish I knew who she was? I hate when that happens.

DAY NINETY-NINE – I may not be moving like I used to, but I'll continue to get up. I may forget what I came into the room for, but I will continue to use my mind. I may not be twenty-one anymore, but I won't complain. It sure beats the alternative.

DAY ONE HUNDRED – The realm of glory is within your reach, speak praise, for His name is holy among all names. As you speak His name toward heaven, He is breathing life into your situation through your workplace and around your family.

DAY ONE HUNDRED-ONE – You will not travel in the same circles of destruction, you are beginning a new season. You will not dwell on your failures, hurt or bitterness; you are beginning a new season. Cast off the cares of this world, put on the breastplate of righteousness, open your arms to God's grace and mercy. You are heading into a new season of deliverance.

DAY ONE HUNDRED-TWO – You should always be yourself. Most will appreciate it. A few will be embarrassed by it. There will be one or two who will hate you for it, but God will applaud it! He has made you the exact way He needs you to be in this moment in time. Embrace Yourself!

Experimental guinea pigs

Years ago I was between jobs. So, I signed up for a case study on experimental drugs for high blood pressure medications – Hey, no judging! I actually made $78.00 doing it, although it cost me $84.00 in gas. Anyway, it was a short study and it was something I had been curious about. I had an appointment early the next day when I noticed my arms and legs were dry. I grabbed some lotion and lathered it on pretty thick. On the way there, I noticed I must have grabbed the perfumed scented lotion.

During the first meeting the staff was getting all my vitals, filling out paperwork to say I wouldn't sue if I dropped dead, and then I was ushered into a room of about twenty-five other people. A quick glance at the group and I could see I was by far the youngest one there, by a good forty years, with the average age being around eighty-five to ninety years old. I heard one gentleman asking the guy next to him who the "kid" was. I grabbed a seat in the front and smiled as everyone filed in.

Okay, within thirty seconds the woman sitting next to me started coughing and gasping for air. I figured she was possibly dying since 90% of them were on oxygen already. All of sudden she yells out, "OMG, someone is wearing scented perfume!" Now I knew I was to blame, but I was too embarrassed to say it was me, so I just looked around at the group wondering who might be blamed. She suddenly looked at me and pointed her very long finger saying, "IT'S YOU!" The teacher tried to calm the woman down, but to no avail, she just kept yelling, coughing and gasping for breath.

I finally cracked under the pressure and said it was me. I told the teacher I would go wipe it off. The teacher apologized again. I kept my head down until I got to the bathroom. I scrubbed and wiped the offending odor off. When I felt I had gotten most of it, I went back to class. When I opened the door, the entire class was sitting on the left, and there was one seat on the right, for me. My advice to you would be to always wear unscented lotions to any experimental drug screenings.

> "Be strong and courageous. Do not be afraid or tremble at them, for the Lord your God is the one who goes with you. He will not fail you or forsake you." Deuteronomy 31:6 (NASB)

WORDS OF ENCOURAGEMENT FOR THE WEEK:

DAY ONE HUNDRED-THREE – I will not let my circumstances define who I am. I will make the choice to follow Him. I will not listen to what I can't do, but what I must do. I have not been forsaken by God. I have not been cast aside, He is my redeemer and I will follow Him all the days of my life.

DAY ONE HUNDRED-FOUR – C H A N G E – Christ reigns inside of them – Heavenly realms surround them – Angels guard their every step – Noble are they that hear the call and move forward – Glorious are their shadows as they begin their day – Excellence starts their journey for their life's calling begin anew. *Dedicated to those who are in the mission field sharing the gospel of Jesus Christ.

DAY ONE HUNDRED-FIVE – You've been given another chance, another moment, another word, make the most of your time, energy, and gifts to help others today. It is not random that you are here. There are no accidents with God. You are where God needs you to be in this moment in time. Stop looking at the situation as the problem, you are better than that. You were made with a purpose. You have a quest to complete. Now focus on what is truly your reason for being today. May God bless you and direct you in the path you are on.

DAY ONE HUNDRED SIX – Every morning my mother opens her blinds, even if it's still dark outside. She said she never wants to miss the sunrise when it comes up over the horizon. This reminds me that I need to keep my heart open, even if it's still dark outside, because if I don't I may miss the sunrise when it comes over the horizon. Don't miss out on the beauty of what God has planned for you because you're blinds are down.

DAY ONE HUNDRED SEVEN – CHANGE will raise up heroes. Change brings about opportunity. Change will take you out of your comfort zone. Change will find out who is ready for the harvest. Change is standing in the crossroad of your destiny. Change will usher in greatness. Prepare yourself to be part of the first responders – God's Hand will be on you. Blessings!

DAY ONE HUNDRED EIGHT – Your life won't be looked upon by what you've owned, but how you gave. Not how many times you've read the Bible, but what you shared in the Bible. Your life won't be looked upon by how many positions you held in the church, but by how many times you shared the gospel of Christ. It is time to change the way we think.

DAY ONE HUNDRED NINE – Are you sad, worried, depressed, anxious, afraid, or scared? How about bitter, angry, or resentful? How's that working for you? Do you find yourself thinking about it every waking moment? I'm not saying you don't have real problems, real concerns, real hurts, but you don't have to carry this burden alone. Bring it to God, all your hurt, anger, and disappointments, bring it all to Him. Praise Him in the storm, before you see any results and thank Him for what He is doing in your life. You were never meant to carry your burdens alone. God wants a relationship with you. He's waiting – go to Him now.

Wow, You're Hot

Ten years ago Ron had bought me a new wallet for Christmas. Inside was a small, taped piece of paper with a drawing of Ron's head and the caption said, "WOW, She's HOT!" Every time I went into my wallet I would see that small scrap of paper, it would always bring a smile to my face.

As with all material things, my wallet eventually wore out and I had to buy a new one. While I was emptying out my old wallet, I took out the scrap of paper and taped it into my new wallet. Of course I was still using the old tape so it wasn't in too securely.

Recently, while making a purchase, I took out my new wallet to pay. As with a new wallet, it is always an adjustment to get used to where everything is. In the process of taking out my money, the small scrap of paper fell on to the register belt. Before I had a chance to grab it, the cashier picked it up and read in a monotone voice, "Wow, she is hot". Then she looked at me, yawning. I smiled and explained that my husband had given me that scrap of paper years ago, reminding me when I was "hot". The cashier, who looked eighteen, was unimpressed. She asked me if I wanted the scrap of paper back. I said "yes" and quickly put it back into the wallet. Oh, and just to make it slightly more embarrassing, there was a line of equally bored young people. Then I dropped my wallet and all my loose change fell out on to the counter. As I left, I thought young people don't have a clue to what sexy is anymore.

SCRIPTURE:

> "Husbands, love your wives, just as Christ loved the church and gave himself up for her." Ephesians 5:25 (NIV)

WORDS OF ENCOURAGEMENT FOR THE WEEK:

DAY ONE HUNDRED-TEN – Many years ago, our oldest, Jessy, was driving home from college. Three hours out, in the middle of the night, her car broke down. Ron drove up to get her. The next day Ron and my dad went back up to get her car. One mile before they get there my father said, "You have the key, right?" Ron sighing deeply says, "you couldn't have asked me that question three hours ago?" Ron, who is usually very laid back and easy going, is feeling the stress of the day. He called the locksmith and prayed there would be an extra set of keys in the glove box. He started to pace as the locksmith approached them. My father, sensing Ron's stress level said, "Ronnie, let me handle this". As Ron goes over to shake the man's hand, my father rattles off the "story". *This may be a good time to mention that as a family we don't do well under stressful situations. Even eating out can be somewhat of a challenge for our family.

"Thank you for coming out," my dad said. "We pulled over on the side of the road because we both had to go to the bathroom at the same time in the woods, leaving the keys in the car." Ron just stares at my dad and thought, "WHAT"? Ron confessed later on to me that he seriously thought about running over to push my dad down. When Ron came home, he told me what happened. I had to laugh and said, "That will teach you for letting dad "handle" it". Ron was grateful that there was an extra set of keys in the glove compartment on that particularly stressful day. I still think this story is funny, and Ron still does not!

DAY ONE HUNDRED-ELEVEN – My problem has been that I was focused on the issue. My problem has been that I was looking for the why. He reminded me this morning that His love for me goes beyond the issues and beyond the whys – His relationship with me is personal. He took great care in making me just the way I am. Trust Him to know what is best for you. For the trials and tribulations we have here on Earth are just a moment in time, but our relationship with Him is eternal – His ways are not our ways. His love for me is overwhelming. I can't stress this enough – HE LOVES YOU!

DAY ONE HUNDRED-TWELVE – You say you are not qualified for the job. You say the odds are against you. You say it simply cannot be done. You say you are outnumbered. You say it has never happened before. You say you don't even know where to begin? According to the Bible, you are perfect for the job. You're hired and may begin immediately.

DAY ONE HUNDRED-THIRTEEN – Do you sometimes have a difficult time hearing God's voice? Do you ever go into panic mode? Where is He? Is He mad? Are you being punished? If you are not careful, this could very well be a time when the devil could wedge into your heart doubt and fear. The silence doesn't mean He does not want to communicate with you, but He will not be forced into your time schedule. You should not confuse the silence with the presence of God in your life. He will never leave or forsake you. Keep your mind open, being ever watchful. When He is ready, He will speak loud and clear into your spirit.

DAY ONE HUNDRED-FOURTEEN – There are some who can only look at their problems or heartache and turn bitter. There are some who stick their head in the sand, denying they have any problems or feel anything at all. There are a few who see their problem as an opportunity to help others, a time to draw closer to God, and a sense of knowing He will bring them through. Which one are you?

DAY ONE HUNDRED-FIFTEEN – Feelings can be deceiving. Go with the promises of God, stay in the Word. Write them down, say them out loud, and memorize them. Next time your emotions start to get the better of you, tell your feelings what God says.

DAY ONE HUNDRED-SIXTEEN – What was the dumbest, the most shocking, and the most fun thing I ever did? Without telling anyone but my husband, the night before, I flew out to Vegas on my own. I hung out with people I had only met online. I was invited and went to Bruce Willis' 50th birthday party. At the age of 47 I got my one and only tattoo; with no regrets and no take backs. Looking back I can definitely see God's angels were protecting me. In spite of making some poor decisions, I met some wonderful and caring ladies who are still my friends today. BW is a very kind and patient man. I suppose everyone has a story or secret that is totally out of character for them. Even though I am in a different place now, it is an important part of my past. I take away with me warm and happy memories. To my KB girls – our friendship means the world to me and I thank God every day for each one of you.

CHAPTER FIVE

BLESS THE LITTLE CHILDREN

The spirit of gambling

One of my in-laws favorite past times was buying scratch off lottery tickets and scratching them off on Sunday afternoon. We happened to be over there for Sunday dinner when she pulled out the cards. She told the kids if they wanted to scratch the numbers off, they could keep the winnings if they won. I really didn't see the harm, since we weren't the ones who purchased the tickets, and hey, if we won, good for us. It seemed harmless. There were about fifty cards and the kids had their penny for scratching. They were so excited to see if they had the "magic" card. I figured I'd scratch one off myself. Nope, I didn't even come close to winning. That was enough for me. I went in the other room to read the paper. Our son Josh was the big winner that day, winning twenty dollars. He felt like a king for the rest of the day. I had to smile at their innocence.

Well, soon enough it was time for church. Since Ron was out of town that week, I piled the kids into the van and headed off to Sunday night service. Now I like sitting as close to the front as possible, so I sat second seat in, center row. My son Jason asked if he could sit in the first pew. He was my little preacher man, so of course I said "yes". When we had finished the singing of the hymns, we sat down. I took out my pen to take notes, when the pastor started his sermon - "The evil spirit of GAMBLING".

As you may know by now, my son Jason was a sensitive little guy. He was the type of kid that if I told him to do something, he did it, not liking any kind of yelling or disciplinary action on our part. So, when the pastor said, "The evil spirit of gambling," my son whipped his head around to me, and on his knees, pointing his finger he said rather loud, "MOM!!!!" Through gritted teeth, flushed with embarrassment, and in a quiet tone, I said, "Turn around and be quiet". Jason was under conviction for sure, but he was taking me down with him and that had to stop. Throughout the sermon, which was one LONG hour, Jason would turn around and look at me, with sympathy in his eyes. I seriously was going to hurt that boy if he didn't stop immediately.

Later in the week I received a letter, from a concerned pew dweller in the church, of places to go for Gambler Anonymous meetings. To this day, I have no idea who sent it.

SCRIPTURE:

"And hope does not put us to shame, because God's love has been poured into our hearts through the Holy Spirit who has been given to us." Romans 5:5 (ESV)

WORDS OF ENCOURAGEMENT FOR THE WEEK:

DAY ONE HUNDRED-SEVENTEEN – There have been days when I totally blew it. I let my anger burst forth, I gossiped, and I was mean-spirited. I was down-right hateful, but I have been given another chance – I woke up! I will look at this new day as confirmation that He still has a plan for my life. That He still believes in me. That God trusts me to make better decisions today. Will you join me?

DAY ONE HUNDRED-EIGHTEEN – There will be some who seem to take such pleasure in hurting others. They plot and scheme, they lie and gossip, and they seem to invent new ways to push our buttons. However, I stand today and say I will not let the actions of others take my joy away. I cannot control what others say and do, but I can pray and simply give the rest to God. Only for a season, stay the course and let God handle what we cannot. He has the final word, stay strong, in time all will be revealed.

DAY ONE HUNDRED-NINETEEN – Even if you know you'll win the fight - what does winning cost you? Pick your battles. Life is too short to be fighting all the time. Author Unknown

DAY ONE HUNDRED-TWENTY – Don't let your life get so busy that it distracts you from loving God, your family, or the stranger you meet today.

DAY ONE HUNDRED TWENTY-ONE – Speak it. Believe it. Release it. Proclaim it. Conquer it. Adore it. Explore it. Light it. Visualize it. Multiply it. Remember it. Embrace it. It's your life, make the moments count. This is your time to shine it!

DAY ONE HUNDRED TWENTY-TWO – Some of the hardest tribulations I have ever had to witness was watching loved ones going through a difficult period in their life. I remember when my son broke his elbow and he was in physical therapy three times a week. It was brutal to listen to him cry out. He didn't understand the angels dressed as therapists were actually there to help him regain use of his right arm. The endless repetition of completing a task, yet the angels persevered on. Keeping the goal always on the prize, knowing they were making him the best he could possibly be. God's ways are not our ways, we just need to trust Him to bring us through so that one day we will be the best we can possibly be too.

DAY ONE HUNDRED TWENTY-THREE – No matter what happened yesterday or last week, today is full of hope and wonder. I will not mess up this perfectly awesome day with any bitterness, anger, or disappointment. I will focus on what is good and what is pure. I will listen for the laughter and follow it. I will be thankful in all things and I know God has a great plan for you too.

Kids are humbling

My oldest was a precocious four year old. You know the type, old beyond their years. Jessy had a tendency to say things at inappropriate times. I had spoken to her on several occasions, stating that we don't always have to say what we're thinking, but she came by it honestly. Our church had been interviewing pastors since the last one had retired. Ron was one of the deacons and it was our turn to have that visiting minister over for Sunday lunch. We were a small church and did not really have the funds to take someone out to eat.

Well, this particular Sunday, the pastor was a rather large man. How large? Large enough to know that he had been blessed with many a comfort meal by Christian families. Okay, maybe his body frame looked a little bit like a weeble wobble. Now if I was thinking this, I knew my oldest was going to mention it.

So on the way home we had the discussion about not hurting people's feelings and that we didn't like the word "FAT". We also said that children should be quiet while grown-ups were talking. "Do you understand?" I asked. She said, "Yes Mommy." But I could almost hear her mind churning around the word "fat". I wasn't 100% convinced she understood, but I thought I would just keep the conversation going and not give my very insightful child a reason to open her mouth. As the visiting pastor came over, we talked about living in Myrtle Beach and what a great place to be stationed, just small talk. My daughter, Jessy, was very quiet, too quiet. What was she up to?

I saw she was mesmerized as she watched his every move, occasionally she would look at me, and I was giving her the don't say it look…it's a universal look all mom's give their kids. Lunch was ready and we sat around the small round table. We said grace then Jessy asked in her very grown up voice, "Mommy, please pass the fat rolls". Do you ever get a pit in your stomach that you know this dinner isn't going to end well? Everything on the kitchen table was FAT. The fat salt, the fat butter, the fat fork, the fat napkin, the fat glass of milk, the fat kitchen table…everything! It was a long dinner, with longer moments of not saying anything, and for someone who can talk about anything; I was at a loss for words.

Thankfully, there was no confrontation and dinner ended. We gave him his pay, and sure he was grateful just to get the heck out of there. I had to ponder the question, should I have said anything to my daughter before hand? Do we let the chips fall where they may or do we try to head a "situation" off ahead of time? I have found with children they will inspire us one minute and humble us the next. Either way they keep us grounded.

"A time to tear, and a time to mend; a time to be silent, and a time to speak." Ecclesiastes 3:7 (NIV)

WORDS OF ENCOURAGEMENT FOR THE WEEK:

DAY ONE HUNDRED TWENTY-FOUR – Welcome in the change of plans. Don't fight the turn of direction or even the misguided steps. These events could bring you to your destiny! It's a place of discovery, a new way of looking at your life, and a new emerging of your spirit. Walk boldly because you never walk alone.

DAY ONE HUNDRED TWENTY-FIVE – I don't have all the answers. I don't always understand the questions. I don't like to see my loved ones suffering. As much as I want to, I can't fix your problems. What I can do is pray for you. What I can do is ask God to direct your path. What I can do is hold your hand, listen and love you. But know this my love, God and God alone is the answer to your problems. God alone will be there when no one else is. God alone knows and understands you better than anyone else. God alone has a plan for your life. Keep your eyes on Him!

DAY ONE HUNDRED TWENTY-SIX – Be someone's superhero today – PRAY for them.

DAY ONE HUNDRED TWENTY-SEVEN – Sometimes, saying or doing things in bulk can lose the meaning of what you're trying to convey. It is memory overload. Let your life speak what they need to hear. I find it amazing how God can use one simple sentence to unlock the message of His word.

DAY ONE HUNDRED TWENTY-EIGHT – I was wrong, will you forgive me? See that wasn't as hard as you thought it would be – try it again.

DAY ONE HUNDRED TWENTY-NINE – I rise early in the morning and I am content. I talk with my friends and I am encouraged. I walk in the garden and I stand amazed. I watch the answered prayer unfolding and I marvel. I read the written Word and I am humbled. I hear the laughter of my grandchildren and I am filled with joy. May today bring you contentment, encouragement, amazement, merriment, and a generous dose of gratefulness.

DAY ONE HUNDRED THIRTY – The day is new and untouched by human hands. Like a canvas not yet painted. Will your painting have bright vivid colors, or will it be muted with soft, gentle and soothing tones? All the colors are on the palette in front of you. Just pick up the brush and begin. The Master has laid everything you need to complete your painting. If you need help, just raise your hand and He will be there to keep your hand steady. He will stay with you until it is completed.

Teasing – Grandma moment

My mother rarely babysat my children, since we lived all over the Country, but there was one particular time when we asked her to watch them for a few hours. During the course of the day my children began teasing each other. At first it seemed pretty harmless but shortly grew to epic proportions of yelling, crying and gnashing of teeth.

My mother sat the children down and began to tell them of a tale many years ago when she was a young girl. It was supper time and her sister raced her yet again to the dinner table. Grandma told my children how angry she felt. So, she decided she would get even. The kids were spell bound. Grandma knew she had peaked their interest. She continued on. She offered the chair out for her sister to sit, but when her sister went to sit down Grandma pulled the chair away. Her sister fell to the floor hurting her tailbone. Grandma, with tears in her eyes went on to say because of teasing, she hurt her sister and she got a spanking from her mother. To this very day she has carried the guilt of teasing. My mother knew she had my children's full attention.

Looking at each of my children she said, "Now, do you see why teasing is so wrong?" My daughter, Jessy, who always had a question on her mind, "Grandma, have you always had that same face?" Realizing my children had missed the entire point of the lesson she simply said, "Alright, get out". As my young children ran out of the room, they began to wonder if Grandma had always had that same face.

Years later I asked the kids what they were thinking. They told me they just could not picture Grandma being a little kid and getting into trouble. I assured them we all were young at one time and with that they laughed and laughed. The more I assured them we were, the more they laughed. Not really the reaction I was hoping for either.

SCRIPTURE:

"Blessed is he whose transgression is forgiven, whose sin is covered." Psalm 32:1 (KJV)

WORDS OF ENCOURAGEMENT FOR THE WEEK:

DAY ONE HUNDRED THIRTY-ONE – Music releases the toxins out of your soul, so that you may begin to praise, to mourn, to be inspired, to create, and to love in ways you never thought were possible. It's the key to unlocking your heart. Ephesians 5:19 and Colossians 3:16 brings out the importance of singing and praising in the church. Keep in mind that your spirit will take on whatever kind of music you are playing. It is that powerful. Therefore, if you need your creative juices flowing, or just want to rid yourself of emotional toxins turn on the music and let your spirit soar.

DAY ONE HUNDRED THIRTY-TWO – Father, open my eyes to where you want me to go. Give my arms the strength to hold the hurting. Direct my feet to the pathway you want me to walk. Guide my mouth with the words I need to say to bring comfort.

DAY ONE HUNDRED THIRTY-THREE – Feelings can deceive, they may even paralyze you to never move forward to your destiny. Feelings were never meant to rule over us as they are fickle, and if we let them, our feelings will become our masters. We were meant for so much more. Even if you don't feel it, push through.

Even if you don't feel well, believe. Even if your feelings over-whelm you, trust God to provide the answers. He will replace your feelings with peace, joy, and understanding. It's a state of mind as feelings are momentary. Trusting God will bring your feelings under control and give you the peace your spirit longs for.

DAY ONE HUNDRED THIRTY-FOUR – I received a letter from our church office asking me to prayerfully consider being mentored. My mother thought that was so nice that they wanted to do that for me, and Lord knows I needed it. Later in the day I reread the letter and I realized I had made a mistake. Instead of being mentored they wanted to know if I could mentor someone in the church. I brought the letter downstairs to show my mother. I said, "I couldn't believe they would ask me". Without hesitation my mother said, "Well Susie, God does use the lowest of the low to do His work." I had to agree, and with all humbleness I accepted. Mom has a way of speaking truth into any situation. God will always shine for His glory. Note: I have a great self esteem, but I also know when God is using me for His glory, not mine.

DAY ONE HUNDRED THIRTY-FIVE – You may have never heard the name Franklin B. Sanborn, but he had an integral part in saving a young girl's life many years ago. He was about to change the course of not just one girls life, but millions of lives due to this one act of kindness. He was simply there to inspect one of the poor houses when a young nine year old girl, with many physi-cal problems ran to him, begging him to let her go to school. He showed mercy on her and because of this one act of kindness, she was taken out of a horrible situation and brought to what her destiny would become. Franklin B. Sanborn saved one child from certain destruction, the girl's name was Anne Sullivan Macy, Helen Keller's teacher. If you ever get the time, I highly recommend you read her autobiography. Will you be a Franklin, an Anne, or maybe a Helen? All were extremely important in helping the next one achieve their destiny in their life. What will your one act of kindness be?

DAY ONE HUNDRED THIRTY-SIX – I can appreciate the laughter because I have cried. I can appreciate my health because I have been sick. I can appreciate the good times because I have had bad. I can appreciate going on vacation because I have been poor. I can appreciate a true friend because I have been betrayed. I can appreciate peace of mind because at one time I had none.

DAY ONE HUNDRED THIRTY-SEVEN – It's not about me was the answer when the doctor said not yet. It's not about me was the answer when I wanted to ask God why. It's not about me was the answer when the prayer seemed to go unanswered. It's all about Him, It's all about His timing, it is all about His perfect plan, and I choose to praise His holy name. He has us all in His merciful hand. Thank you God for loving me right where I am!

The witch

It was our stewardship banquet night at the church. We had been raising money to build our new church building in the late summer. We had gotten a babysitter for the older three, but thought we should keep Jenni with us, especially since she had a real talent for taking off when no one was watching. We sat across from a nice couple and were enjoying ourselves and the evening. All of a sudden Jenni, who was usually very shy, and spoke so softly, looked across the table and said, "Mommy, she looks like the wicked witch of the west". I swear her punctuation was clear and perfectly stated. I mean, holy smokes, the lady did have an uncanny resemblance to the wicked witch of the west. I think it was the chin. Why did I let the kids watch *The Wizard of Oz*?

I went into panic mode. I did what any young mother of four would do, I made pretend I didn't hear her. Now she was pointing at the lady, "Mommy, she looks like the wicked witch of the west, and I'm scared". Oh Lord, I prayed, it is okay with me if the rapture comes right now. I AM READY! Amen.

I simply was at a loss for words. I just kept looking away hoping beyond hope no one else heard her. "What did your little girl say?" "Um, I don't know, I can't understand a word she says", I answered. "Did she say I look like a witch?" "Oh did she?" I replied again. "She says that about everyone, they just watched *The Wizard of Oz*, so now we're all the wicked witch of the west witches, wacky, crazy kids", I nervously chuckled. I remember thinking, why did we teach our kids to talk again?

SCRIPTURE:

"Set a guard, O Lord, over my mouth; keep watch over the door to my lips." Psalm 141:3 (NIV)

WORDS OF ENCOURAGEMENT FOR THE WEEK:

DAY ONE HUNDRED THIRTY-EIGHT – You were meant to be extraordinary, not ordinary. Plan accordingly.

DAY ONE HUNDRED THIRTY-NINE – May I always be appreciative and not attacking, compassionate and not controlling, uplifting and not down hearted, joyful and not anxious, victorious and not discouraging, loving, but not jealous. With each positive there is always a negative. Time to re-program how and why we think.

DAY ONE HUNDRED FORTY – You are the one. You have been hand-picked. Your DNA says so. Nothing compares to what you will bring forth to the table. You were made with one purpose under heaven. What difference will your life make on this world? Get ready – stay steady – it's you.

DAY ONE HUNDRED FORTY-ONE – You should prepare yourself. Just before you experience a breakthrough, or are on the verge of an awakening, or just as greatness is coming your way. You may experience illness, heart break, or financial problems may come into your life. God has not forgotten you. The devil is just throwing everything he can to get your eyes off of God and on your situation. Take your stand, stay focused, and know that God Almighty stands with you.

DAY ONE HUNDRED FORTY-TWO – I may have started out weak but with God at my side I'll be crossing the finish line strong and victorious.

DAY ONE HUNDRED FORTY-THREE – Speak about not being fair – We give God all our anger, bitterness and hatred and He gives us all His love, mercy and grace. Fairness has nothing to do with it – Thank God!

DAY ONE HUNDRED FORTY-FOUR – We, as a society, will do almost anything to achieve physical perfection. Go through any surgical procedure to take a few years off our ever aging bodies. We are always looking for the next miracle pill or cream. The question begs to be asked, at least by me, "What about our spiritual bodies?" Show kindness and compassion to keep skin soft and youthful. Be the strongest in your neighborhood by prayers and supplication. Forgiveness and love will define the abs you've always wanted. Walk with humility and your legs will be long and strong. Seek salvation and eternal beauty will be yours forever. Exercise by reading the Word of God every day. Let your hair shine with the glory of God.

The Prostitute

The year my husband was overseas on a remote, we moved in with my parents. We also thought it would be a great time for all three generations to come together under one roof. During one particular Saturday evening, my dad was talking about helping out at a shelter in downtown Worcester. He was a member of the Knights of Columbus so he volunteered a lot of time with the Special Olympics and soup kitchens. The kids listened intently. I usually sent them outside to play when the grown-ups were talking, but I thought it was educational for them to hear about helping others in need. Dad went on to say that there were all kinds of people that were going through a difficult time. The homeless, drug addicts, and even the prostitutes came in for a free cup of soup on a chilly evening.

The next day was Sunday and it was nice that the older two were now at an age where they would accompany me into the main church sanctuary. After the morning service, the pastor was out shaking everyone's hand. Jason was just in front of me when the pastor took his hand and shook it while saying, "young man, I'm sure you are a big help to your mom while your dad's away." Jason spoke right up, "yes sir, I want to take care of her so she doesn't have to live with the prostitutes in Worcester."

Now the pastor's eyes got big as saucers and even though he never said anything, I wondered if he was thinking, "how does a nine year old know the word prostitute or was he shocked that I may become one in the near future?" I would have scolded Jason on the way home, but the damage had already been done. This was the same church where everyone thought I had a gambling problem too. Besides, it was true, I hope I never become a prostitute and become a burden to my family.

SCRIPTURE:

> "But Joshua spared Rahab the prostitute, with her family and all who belonged to her, because she hid the men Joshua had sent as spies to Jericho – and she lives among the Israelites to this day." Joshua 6:25 (NIV)

WORDS OF ENCOURAGEMENT FOR THE WEEK:

DAY ONE HUNDRED FORTY-FIVE – A few years ago Ron and I had gone out to dinner. As Ron looked across the table he could tell I was preoccupied with the cares of the world. I was staring off when Ron took my hand and said, "What is on your mind?" I didn't want to bother him with all my thoughts and concerns but he insisted I share my burdens and worldly cares with him. He said we had been married all these years and if something was bothering me, it bothered him too. So I did. After two hours, I felt a tremendous burden had been lifted from me. Ron leaned in and quietly said, "Remind me to never ask you that question again!" Well I busted out laughing. I am not saying don't share your heart with your spouse, but only God can truly help you overcome all your problems, insecurities, frustrations and heart-ache. People can help you to a point, but they are not meant to help with every small detail. Only God can handle whatever is on your mind and in your heart, all the time. When the burdens become too much, bring it all to Him, for His yolk is light, and He is always available to hear you.

DAY ONE HUNDRED FORTY-SIX – Have you ever connected with someone instantly? They are your kindred spirits, you feel like you have known them forever. I believe God ordained certain people into our lives, and our spirit recognizes them, to be there for us no matter the circumstances. They are crucial in our walk on this earth.

DAY ONE HUNDRED FORTY-SEVEN – Let my spirit become strong by reading Your Word daily. Let my heart stay tender by serving those around me. Let my mind remain pure by dwelling on what is good and kind and holy. Let my body reflect Your temple by nurturing a wholesome life style.

DAY ONE HUNDRED FORTY-EIGHT – Never under estimate the power of prayer. Never minimize the kindness of words. Never under value the strength of a gentle touch. Never miscalculate how important positive thinking is during a crisis. Never lose encouragement where the heart is involved.

DAY ONE HUNDRED FORTY-NINE – I love the tapestry of my life. The intricate patterns that weave my story. All the many colors that have formed pathways from bright to dark, to pastels, and muted tones. The thread is strong and I see where I have re-enforced the edges, so not to lose the continual story being told. My tapestry covers my home with love, even though I may not have chosen all the colors, and I have been tempted to rip out the ugly sections. Yet, there is no denying that some of the prettiest designs are when the dark and the light colors overlap one another.

DAY ONE HUNDRED FIFTY – "Show me a hero and I'll write you a tragedy." By F. Scott Fitzgerald – If every day was wonderful, there would be no need for heroes. Stay the course, God is not finished with you yet.

DAY ONE HUNDRED FIFTY-ONE – Nana moment: We had brought our grandsons, Jake and Vinny, to Chuck E. Cheese for the first time while on vacation. I had no idea that Vinny was terrified of heights until he got way up in that "gerbil maze" that kids like to climb into. I could see Vinny's face was starting to panic, so I told Jake to go up and get his little brother. There were many large windows which told us that Vinny was now in full panic mode and Jake was beside himself with what to do. The horror I felt being so helpless on the ground. I found a worker who I expressed my sense of urgency to help us. He on the other hand was not sensing my urgency and told me he would get someone to help, as he looked around completely disinterested.

He was speaking to the wrong Nana. I told him that he would be perfect for the job, and hoisted him up into the maze, within minutes we were reunited with Vinny and Jake. My heart was racing and I began to wonder if we had scarred him for life when Vinny tugged on my sleeve asking if he could please have some more tokens to play games.

CHAPTER SIX

THE JOYS OF PARENTHOOD

Keeping your hands busy

The doctor said, "Your son will need to have surgery." "The break is complicated. So, we may have to put in screws and rods to hold the bone in place." The last thing I wanted to hear on that chilly, October evening in Minot, North Dakota. Funny the thoughts that comes to your mind when a crisis arises. Earlier in the evening, I remember talking to Jason about why I liked to work on needle point. I told him I enjoyed making pretty things for our home, and I remember my mother saying that her grandfather told her that keeping your hands busy left no room for mischief and getting into trouble. I always tried to provide some type of learning while talking to the children about why we do the things we do.

I was cleaning up the supper dishes while the kids and Ron were outside playing at the neighbor's house. Our oldest daughter, Jessy, came running in, yelling, "Mom, Jason got hurt." Apparently the kids were playing football, and Jason jumped on the older boys back to tackle him down, but the boy flipped Jason over him. While trying to brace for the fall, Jason kept his arm straight. When he crashed down the elbow shattered. We couldn't be certain if his growth plate had been injured or not until they got in there to open him up. Jason seemed so small in that big hospital bed and I wasn't about to leave his side.

We were blessed with an amazing church family who took care of the other kids. After much prayer, it turned out that Jason's growth plate had been spared. The break was still severe, but he was going to be okay. I had Ron bring me my needle-point to pass away the long hours at the hospital. Jason was in and out of sleeping until the doctor came in to check on his little patient. The doctor, trying to make small talk, asked me what I was making and if I enjoyed working on needlepoint. Before I had a chance to open my mouth, Jason, who was fully awake now said, "My mom needs to work on needlepoint all the time or her hands start to do evil things". My face wore the look of shock, mortification, and utter disbelief. The doctor was silent for only a few moments, but really, how does one recover from those kinds of comments? I tried to explain, but I felt like it was all in vain. How does working hands are happy hands, vs. I must keep my hands busy or evil will be done? I don't know, but that was the last needlepoint pillow I ever made. For some reason it just wasn't fun anymore.

SCRIPTURE:

"Lazy hands make for poverty, but diligent hands bring wealth." Proverbs 10:4 (NIV)

WORDS OF ENCOURAGEMENT FOR THE WEEK:

DAY ONE HUNDRED FIFTY-TWO – Being the first to forgive doesn't make you weak, it just means you are letting God move you to the next level of greatness.

DAY ONE HUNDRED FIFTY-THREE – Lord, let me hear your voice today. Cover my mouth so that I may not sin. Guard my steps in the path I choose to walk today. Quiet my mind so I may know your will. Open my eyes to see those in need. Bring joy into my heart regardless of my present circumstances. Dear Father, most of all give me the courage to make you proud!

DAY ONE HUNDRED FIFTY-FOUR – Lord, may I have the perseverance to carry on the good fight, ignoring the intolerance of others. Give me forbearance in worldly matters, while speaking reassurance to those in need, and open Your arms for deliverance.

DAY ONE HUNDRED FIFTY-FIVE – Your life is not a dress rehearsal, what are you waiting for?

DAY ONE HUNDRED FIFTY-SIX – If it's not you - than who will go?

DAY ONE HUNDRED FIFTY-SEVEN – Our heavenly Father
He knew your worth,
before your birth.
He knows your pain,
but keeps you sane.
He comes to you throughout the day.
It's up to you to let Him stay.
He fights your battles in the dark,
while you sleep He gently rocks.
Trust in Him in all you do,
for peace and joy will follow you!

DAY ONE HUNDRED FIFTY-EIGHT – Are you ready to run the race? Do you want to finish strong? I know the best coach. He will get you focused. He will run beside you. He will encourage you and He will meet you as you cross the finish line. Let

God be your life coach. Everyone He has coached has become a champion!

Toot. Toot, toot, jingle all the way

While visiting our son Josh over the Christmas holiday, I was reminded how men are really just little boys who happen to shave every day. I don't know how it is in your house, but I have found that the men in our family just really don't care for shopping. I told Ron and Josh that I would move more quickly if they weren't with me and that we would meet up at Bed, Bath and Beyond. I watched them dragging their feet as they went on their way. Two sad little men walking away, besides they were "dead weight" around my quick shopping abilities.

As I entered Bed, Bath, and Beyond, I almost felt overwhelmed with the large crowds of Christmas shoppers. I decided I would just stroll up and down each aisle, I mean how hard could it be to find them? Josh was a military man himself now and Ron kind of looked like the snowman from *Rudolph the Red-nose Reindeer*, classic Christmas cartoon. I started to hum to myself, silver and gold, silver and gold...hum, hum, hum, hum, hum, hum, silver and gold. All of a sudden my thoughts were interrupted by farting noises. What a mood breaker that was. Where was it coming from? Not only farting noises, but it was farting out a tune, jingle bells, jingle bells, jingle all the way... toot, toot, toot, toot, toot, toot, toot, toot, toot, toot, toot!

As I got closer to the obnoxious noise, I heard two men laughing hysterically and the sad part was I recognized them. The farts were coming from my beloved husband and grown son. That's right, they had found the whoopee cushion section, seriously, who even buys those kinds of presents anymore? I went right up to them both and said, "STOP," immediately both just tooted on their whoopee's and laughed even harder. Had they no respect? It's one thing behind closed doors, but quite another at Bed, Bath, and Beyond. I noticed people were looking at us, judging us, shaking their heads slightly in disgust of our tooting ways. I again pleaded with my husband, who was in his mid fifty's, and my adult son, who was in the military. They looked at me and let out the biggest TOOT of all...and again, laughed beyond reason. I decided there was nothing else I could do.

I mustered up all the self respect I could gather and walked away. Upon leaving the area, the "boys" tooted one more time and said, "gee lady, you could at least say excuse me", laughing till they cried. I didn't know whether I was blessed or humbled, or both, but in spite of their toots we managed to have a wonderful Christmas season.

SCRIPTURE:

"But God chose what is foolish in the world to shame the wise; God chose what is weak in the world to shame the strong. God chose the lowly things of this world and the despised things and the things that are not – to nullify that things that are, so that no one may boast before him."
1 Corinthians 1: 27-29 (NIV)

DAY ONE HUNDRED FIFTY-NINE – Traveling on Route 81 during the autumn is a sight to behold. The colors are vibrate, the air is crisp and cool, and watching nature burst forth one last time with a beauty unmatched in any other time of the year. I was reminded that even though I am in the autumn of my life, it is not a time to slow down, but to gear up and give it everything I have. I will not rest today because soon enough winter will be here.

DAY ONE HUNDRED SIXTY – Do you assume? Assuming can bite you in the butt. Assuming can hurt your feelings. Assuming can let your guard down. Assuming can open the door to prejudice. Assuming everything you read or see is a fact. Assuming can be frustrating and rob you of true joy. Pray that God will open your eyes to His truth, His ways, His love for your life.

DAY ONE HUNDRED SIXTY-ONE – My life as a tree – My trunk is growing ever upwards to feel the sun on my bark. The branches are my family and friends, helping me stay balanced. My leaves are my children and grandchildren. Each one is unique and adds beauty to my frame. My roots are my relationship with Christ, digging ever deeper into the rich soil and keeping me well grounded.

DAY ONE HUNDRED SIXTY-TWO – Stepping out in faith can be one of the scariest decisions you ever make. After all, there may be no evidence to support what you are about to do. Logically it's impossible. Faith expects a lot from us. It is a voice which speaks directly to our hearts, can we trust it? Faith wants us to believe in the impossible. Faith has no problem letting us be exposed to ridicule by the world. Faith comes at a price and the price is high. It requires self control, it requires patience, it requires belief in the super natural, and it demands every part of us. So why have it? Faith will lift you to places you never thought were possible. Faith will restore your physical, mental, and spiritual being. Faith will bring you peace. Faith will show the world, even without the physical evidence, because of your Faith the impossible came to pass. Prayer and Faith go hand in hand – if you have both of these in your spirit you can do anything! Did you hear me? ALL THINGS ARE POSSIBLE!

DAY ONE HUNDRED SIXTY-THREE – Never assume - when it comes to how God answers prayer. I have found He has a unique way of getting His point across in changing the hearts, the circumstances, and our faith. Can you imagine, most times He won't even give us a heads up – That's right, He's that good!

DAY ONE HUNDRED SIXTY-FOUR – What is keeping you from serving the Lord? It's time to get off the fence, jump out of your seat, stand up and walk down the aisle; the harvest is ready my friend. We are living in a day that is ripe – this is the season of harvest!

DAY ONE HUNDRED SIXTY-FIVE – We must weather the storms together. We are warriors in a wild and unpredictable world. One minute it will be warm and wonderful, the next will bring wild winds and whipping rains. Why is one day so predictable, while another so wacky and weird? When the time is right we will gain wisdom and wonder how we could have ever been so wrong and willful. Let us work together and not wither on the vine. Wake up, we need to tell the weak there is hope, we need to pray for wise counsel, and worship our Lord every Wednesday, for His wonder is beyond our wildest dreams.

This message was brought to you by the letter W.

And the winner is

The year was 1988 and we were in yet another presidential election. We happened to be up north at the time, Ron was deployed yet again. The two parties were between the Republican, George Bush Sr., and Democrat, Michael Dukakis. But I'm getting ahead of myself. My parents were enjoying the time I was there since being in the military usually took us far away, but my kids were still little and were still needy. Sometimes this proved to be somewhat of a balancing act between my parents and my young children.

My dad told the kids that I needed some "alone" time without them interrupting, and just to sweeten the pot my Dad brought out his old Knights of Columbus return envelopes, paper with his official letterhead on top, poster boards, pieces of wood, hammer, nails, and told them to build Grandpa something amazing. Guess what? It worked. The kids were busy all afternoon, my father was in his glory. "See," he said, "you just have to know how to handle kids."

Throughout the afternoon we would hear occasional horns beeping and the kids yelling. I decided I had had enough "grown-up time," back to reality and check on the kids. As I looked out the living room window, much to my trepidation, my kids had taken the poster boards, nailed them to the boards and were holding them up as cars drove by. Vote for George Bush because Michael Dukakis is a stupid head. Now you have to understand, in my parent's day you never discussed sex, religion or politics, EVER. Not to mention my parents were die hard democrats, or that their neighbor was actually friends with Dukakis and was serving on his political team.

I saw my life flash in front of my eyes. I also saw my dad's life flash in front of my eyes too. Now, when Dad was really mad, he didn't make a lot of sense, just a lot of stuttering and swearing. Oh yes, the choice swearing that only Dad could do. I couldn't get out there fast enough to clean up and get the kids to come inside. As the kids single filed back into the house, my father had finally calmed down, seeing that the kids weren't trying to give us all a heart attack.

As I looked at each face, from oldest to youngest, I said, "So, now you understand, you do not hold up any more signs that say mean things about people." My mom added that "who people vote for is very private and not to be discussed." Jessy, the oldest, said, "oh that's okay Grandma, we won't do that anymore, we let everyone know who to vote for when we put our letters in everyone's mailbox." "What did you put in everyone's mailbox?" I asked. "We used the paper and envelopes that Grandpa gave us and told everyone to vote for George Bush." Now I looked slowly over to dad to see him opening his mouth, and closing, open and close, no words came out. He just kept opening and closing. Mom just kept blessing herself with the sign of the cross. I guess we may have overstayed our welcome.

"For we all stumble in many ways. And if anyone does not stumble in word, he says, he is perfect man, able to bridle his whole body." James 3:2 (NKJV)

WORDS OF ENCOURAGEMENT FOR THE WEEK:

DAY ONE HUNDRED SIXTY-SIX – BEWARE: The devil tries to mirror God in all ways, but he will always fall short. The devil will deceive and cover up. God will speak the truth and expose it out. The devil will make the outside look all shiny and new, but on the inside it is dark full of cobwebs, and there is no substance. God chooses the plain, the unassuming, the simple, and transforms them into His masterpiece. Man-made material will always corrode but the miracles of God will endure forever. God's beauty is different than the world's definition of beauty. A perfect example of this would be how many people try to have the perfect face and body through plastic surgery only to find they are never content and keep trying until their face is horribly disfigured. Remember the devil's creation will lie and give empty promises of love and self adoration. God will bring your natural beauty out and set you above all others. Look in, not out.

DAY ONE HUNDRED SIXTY-SEVEN – Trying to get through the day without God is like trying to put on a girdle without arms.

DAY ONE HUNDRED SIXTY-EIGHT – While watching SOME recent Christian television shows, I have noticed a disturbing trend towards saying if people will just send in a certain amount of money, God will show them favor, God will heal them, and God will protect them from all bad things. YIKES! Is this true?

Not from what I have read in the Bible. Now don't misunderstand me, God does want to bless us. He does heal and He does protect us, but it is not a trade off or by doing good works that in it self will bring us favor with God. He loves us right where we are. He is giving, He is merciful, and He will never leave or forsake us. In II Corinthians 4:8-11, 12:10, I Peter 4:12-19, 5:10 and Romans 5:3-5, tell us that His people will have suffering, that we will go through tribulation and heartache, BUT God says to rejoice, be strong, be content, have hope for our ultimate rewards will be in heaven. All according to His will. God will use the tribulations and heartache to mold us into the people we are meant to become. He will bless not because of who we are, but because of who He is. With this said, if you feel led to send in a donation to help a ministry do so, but don't expect to win the lottery because of your good works.

DAY ONE HUNDRED SIXTY-NINE – I used to focus in on the problems, believing if I could figure out all the angles that I could somehow protect my loved ones and myself. What I was actually doing was bringing up some good old fashioned pride; no faith, no trust. The only thing I was able to accomplish was to stress and worry myself out. The day I repented and gave it to God was the day my spirit found rest, peace of mind, and joy of heart.

DAY ONE HUNDRED SEVENTY – Next time you pray for it try something different – stop complaining!

DAY ONE HUNDRED SEVENTY-ONE – Activate the Power of God – Meditate on the positive - Rejoice in the possibilities – Walk with the knowledge that you never walk alone. What begins in the mind will manifest into your life.

DAY ONE HUNDRED SEVENTY-TWO – Dear Monday,
It has come to my attention that you like to throw a wrench into your week. You like to cause mischief and depression wherever you go. I heard you have made it your goal in life to turn off people's morning alarm clocks making them late for work. This must stop immediately! You do not own the week. You are not in charge just because you are Monday. You will treat people with respect and fall in line with the other days. You do not want me to call Sunday. I have let the rest of the week know that you are on probation. Now straighten up, and remember who you are – the cornerstone of the week! Let this day bring you hope, joy and a new beginning!

Follow your nose

As clean as I tried to keep the house, the boy's bedroom was a challenge for me. There was a distinct odor coming from that room in the summer of '86. It started to get so bad that just walking by the room was enough to make us gag. That's it, the kids were at swimming lessons, and Jenni was taking a nap. I put on my yellow rubber gloves and grabbed my cleaning bucket and supplies. I striped the beds, I sanitized, I scrubbed, and yet, the smell was still there.

What was that odor? I stood in the middle of the room and started to sniff. That's right, like a beagle. Not one of my finest moments. The last thing was the bureau. I opened each drawer and took in a big whiff, while sweat was pouring off me, since it was the one of the hottest days of the summer. Finally, I came to the bottom of their bureau drawer. Yes it was here, I was close, ripping out papers, underwear, crayons, a piece of candy, broken toy soldiers, and finally a gray sport sock. I picked it up. There it was and something was in it. Was it a dead animal? I put the end of the sock up to my face, put my nose in and sniffed deeply... big mistake, I swear it smelled so bad that I almost went flying across the room.

With my mouth and nose now covered with a hand towel, I turned the sock upside down and out it came...an Easter egg from April. To this day I have never smelled anything worse than that egg. When the boys came home from swimming lessons we sat down and had a talk. They seemed upset that I had taken and thrown away their precious egg! Where do little boys come from?

SCRIPTURE:

"Behold, children are a heritage from the Lord, the fruit of the womb is a reward. Happy is the man who fills his quiver full of them. He shall not be ashamed, but shall speak with his enemies in the gate." Psalm 127: 3-5. (NKJV)

WORDS OF ENCOURAGEMENT FOR THE WEEK:

DAY ONE HUNDRED SEVENTY-THREE – "Are we there yet?" A parents most hated sentence on a long trip. Our travels would usually start out great, the adventure of the unknown, making sure we were prepared for all situations, maps, food, water, games, but inevitably about half way there, if we were lucky, the kids would start whining and arguing, getting into the other child's "space". After they would torture each other, they would bring us into it. I remember one time when our son Josh, who was eight, kept saying "good day mate" for SIX hours, just to torment his sister Jenni. The only thing that kept Josh alive during that time is that my seat belt held me in place so I couldn't quite reach him. We would eventually end up at our destination, but we looked like we had been through the battle. When you are on a life journey, do you start off with all kinds of hope and excitement only to get discouraged and angry half way through? Do you ever ask God, "are we there yet?" over and over? It's time to move into the front seat and become a spiritual adult.

DAY ONE HUNDRED SEVENTY-FOUR – He made the earth by His power, He founded the universe by his wisdom, and He stretched out the heavens by His understanding…do I think He can help me with my problem? Are you kidding me? YES, YES I do!

DAY ONE HUNDRED SEVENTY-FIVE – "Do you want to be powerful? – pray!" By Mother Theresa

DAY ONE HUNDRED SEVENTY-SIX – You could live in the biggest homes, own expensive cars, live in the best neighborhood, send your kids to the most prestigious schools, and have a retirement fund that would be the envy of everyone from work, but without love you're bankrupt. Everything else will corrode, but love is eternal. We need to start saving for the things that matter in this life and the next one.

DAY ONE HUNDRED SEVENTY-SEVEN – Grateful
Grateful fills my spirit now
humbled on my knees I bow.

Grateful is my state of mind
seeking God just in time.
Sweetness is the answered prayer
there is nothing that quite compares.
I will proclaim it night and day
if only one is saved this way.
Keep my heart so tender dear
in His time all will appear.
I will embrace my Lord today
because I know He is the way!

DAY ONE HUNDRED SEVENTY-EIGHT – "Good morning, I am the new sales representative for a new line of beauty aids I would like you to try. Please sit down and just relax. First, I would love for you to try a new foundation that compliments any skin tone. It is called the Living Water. Living Water, will cleanse out any hidden dirt particles you may still have in the pores of your face. Oh my, you look refreshed already. Now let's see, you need a lipstick that will compliment your mouth, to make it full and young looking. Here it is, it's called Smiling with Ease. This particular brand comes in 3 colors, compliment casual, laugh often, and my favorite, sweet salvation. Ahhh, I can see the changes already. You simply must try our new eyeliner, it is called Kindness Captures the Heart. You can wear this all day long and not have to worry about it smudging off. Now, one last finishing touch, we need to add a little sparkle to those cheeks. I would like to gently brush a light stroke of Humbly I Come. Seriously, the men in your life will just swoon over you. With each purchase made today you get a free gift, The Old Rugged Cross. What I love about this gift is that you can wear it casually or dress it up. Now, look in the mirror. You are a masterpiece! Come back anytime you feel the need to freshen up."

DAY ONE HUNDRED SEVENTY-NINE – What is your family hearing from your mouth? What is your legacy? Whatever you may be experiencing is temporary – everyone gets discouraged, but don't let the discouragement become who you are – you're worth is so much more than that.

CHAPTER SEVEN

LOVING PEOPLE WHERE THEY ARE

Seeing red

I was one of the managers on duty that early spring afternoon. We were having our semi-annual dress sale. I had selected my beautiful red suit with matching floral scarf to work that day. One of our sales associates was getting off work and told me she had been helping a customer with some items. I went directly to where she was and asked her through a closed door if she needed assistance. The lady responded back "yes," she needed a couple more dresses for church, in a size 12, something modest and definitely no RED. She went on to say that red was the devil's color and she wasn't going to wear that devil color to her church. There was another lady going into the next dressing room that gave me a look up and down, and said in a quiet tone, "good luck".

Now, since I was wearing a red suit I didn't know if I should run, feel convicted, or be ashamed. I decided to stick it out and went and got her a few more dresses. As she opened the door, she also looked me up and down. She immediately went into damage control, stating that was really her husband that believed that, and her church frowned on that color, but she was really okay with it. Well, now she was just really starting to irritate me. I didn't miss a beat either, and simply said that I too was a

Christian and that I believed that God made all the colors of the world, including red. I then said how you wear your clothing either suggestive or modest, brings either glory or sin into what you are wearing and not the color. I heard the lady in the next room giggle and say amen. Love them where they are oh Lord, love them where they are!

SCRIPTURE:

"Judge not and you shall not be judged; Condemn not, and you shall not be condemned. Forgive and you will be forgiven." Luke 6:37 (NKJV)

WORDS OF ENCOURAGEMENT FOR THE WEEK:

DAY ONE HUNDRED EIGHTY – As the sun begins rising up over the horizon, the birds start singing to their young, and the smell of coffee travels up to my bedroom. The Lord whispers in my ear, time to rise up and begin again.

DAY ONE HUNDRED EIGHTY-ONE – My Comforter My Lord
I had built a tower of confusion,
I had suffered in my pain
I felt so unworthy,
to even call His name.
I could not find the peace I craved
I could not lift my head.
When I was at my worst,
He was by my bed.
He took my heart and cradled me,
beside the river stream.
When I looked up,
all I could see was glory in the beams.

Now I am strong through Him I found
He was going to stay
I will not rest until they know
He is the only way.

DAY ONE HUNDRED EIGHTY-TWO – I was watching an old *Twilight Zone* episode where an airline inspector was riddled with guilt with unanswered questions on a missing air flight. At one point he even imagines the ghost of the plane comes to his hangar, now empty of any passengers. It was the only case he was never able to solve in his twenty five years of service. He ends up having a nervous breakdown by the end of the show. It got me thinking, there are some questions that won't be answered until we get to heaven. You can go over a problem again and again, and still the answers won't be there. Stop torturing yourself with the what ifs – trust that God knows and leave it with Him.

DAY ONE HUNDRED EIGHTY-THREE – I used to live in Denialville, which you may have heard is the place to go if you live your life in limbo land. We even lived on Prohibition Lane, but our Neighborhood Association was forbidding us to ever try anything new. I tried to join the PTA but their refusal to accept new members was frustrating. Everybody seemed to look the same, no one stood out. In fact the entire town seemed repulsed by anyone who was different from them. The mayor's favorite daily task was to veto and disregard any new ideas that came across his desk. Denialville sounded so good on paper – no worries, no fighting, everyone minds their own business, ideal for raising a family. The flyer should have had a disclaimer that read, "no one commits, rejection is common, and refusal to see the truth is their core belief". The best decision I ever made was to move out of Denialville. Join me today as we begin a new chapter together.

DAY ONE HUNDRED EIGHTY-FOUR – These are not the times to crack and give up. These are the times to trust and obey. These are not the times to question and surrender. These are the times to answer and charge ahead. These are not the times to complain and argue. These are the times to praise and stand together. I am grateful for the day, grateful for the hour, and grateful He is with me now.

DAY ONE HUNDRED EIGHTY-FIVE – <u>Nana moment:</u> When our oldest grandson, Jake, finally understood the concept that we were his Dad's mommy and daddy, he called me on the phone one day and told me that his daddy would not let him do something and could I please put him in timeout. If only it were that easy. Thank you Lord for the gift of laughter and innocence through my grandson, Jake.

DAY ONE HUNDRED EIGHTY-SIX – Expect the best – Believe it will happen – Trust in Him – Visualize it daily – Imagine the difference – Contemplate the choices – Envision the dream – Behold the day!

Very important tip for car passengers

When someone else is driving you do not want to scream or yell out. It is very dangerous and can lead to a disagreement with your loved ones. But in my defense, we had just pulled into our street when I heard a loud thud. I looked up and saw on the windshield a komodo dragon on my side of the windshield. Ron said it was just a chameleon but we both agreed it was HUGE. It must have fallen out of the tree and landed on us as we drove by. It stuck to our windshield like a trooper, not going from the left or to the right, but holding on for all it was worth.

When we pulled in to the driveway, it was still clinging on for dear life. No way was I getting out. So I just continued yelling and screaming, which is very important in a time of crisis. Ron got out and found an ice scraper brush in the garage and gently pushed it off. Upon hitting the grass it got up on its two back legs, like something you would see in a scary movie, and scurried into our neighbor's yard. When I got out of the car, I told Ron my blood pressure must be super high and he said no matter what mine was, his was higher…my bad. I guess looking back I may have over reacted, but it was wicked gross. On a side note I was glad we were still able to use the ice scrapper while living down south.

SCRIPTURE:

"Be not afraid of sudden fear, neither of the desolation of the wicked, when it cometh, for the Lord shall be thy confidence, and shall keep thy foot from being taken." Proverbs 3:25, 26 (KJV)

WORDS OF ENCOURAGEMENT FOR THE WEEK:

DAY ONE HUNDRED EIGHTY-SEVEN – Stop, drop, and kneel; in case of a spiritual fire.

DAY ONE HUNDRED EIGHTY-EIGHT – You want a breakthrough in your life? You must be willing to be broken spiritually – don't stop believing during that season of testing and trials. Stay in prayer and fasting until your breakthrough comes. With each level brings a greater price and a greater reward. A greater humbleness and a greater joy. A greater poverty and a greater wealth. Stay the course, you are not alone!

DAY ONE HUNDRED EIGHTY-NINE –Doubt is the first cousin to fear. Fear is the auntie to worry. Worry is the mother to bitterness. Bitterness is the sister to hate. Hate is the brother to the devil. This family is bad news. Do not let your kids play with them and never invite them over. They will never leave on their own. It is time to clean your house out.

DAY ONE HUNDRED NINETY – The one thing about moms is that we will always be your mom first. You might think that because you are grown up you can now share things you did with your friends, or the trouble you got in to at school, prepare yourself, we will not be amused. As your mom, we want you happy, Lord knows we want that, but we also want to protect you mentally, physically and spiritually. We can't help it. We don't have the luxury of being the friend, because we will forever be your mom. Loving, hard, caring, devoted, a little crazy, but always, always having your best interest in our heart. Author unknown

DAY ONE HUNDRED NINETY-ONE – Our ways are not God's ways, His answers are different than our questions, His timing is not on our calendars…being in prayer, waiting for His direction.

DAY ONE HUNDRED NINETY-TWO – Life is not the planned events, but rather life is full of interruptions, side roads, and back alleys. The interruptions will give us patience, the side roads will show us endurance, and back alleys will keep us humble. Enjoy your life with all its twists and turns, for it will be quite the ride traveled down the road.

DAY ONE HUNDRED NINETY-THREE – If you live long enough, there will eventually be somebody who doesn't like you – just because you talk too much, you're too silly, you're not spiritual enough, or maybe it's just as simple as you talk funny. These have been some of the reasons why people haven't liked me. We are not meant to have EVERYBODY love us. When I was younger it bothered me more, but now I realize that no matter how bad my day is or how much I irritate others, God loves me right where I am and He loves you too! He made you exactly perfect to do what has to be done in your journey in this life.

DAY ONE HUNDRED NINETY-FOUR – What is the secret to losing ten pounds overnight? Forgive someone.

Knock, knock, who's there?

It was an early morning, just before Thanksgiving, when our son Josh came into our bedroom to use the bathroom. He was home on military leave and his little sister was occupying the main bathroom getting ready for work. Now Ron was getting ready for work, and I was not sleeping, but still only vaguely aware of my surroundings. Josh asked if Dad was in the bathroom, because he really had to go. I mumbled out, "just knock first". Well, it had been a long time since we had kids of any age that needed to use the bathroom, especially urgently.

So he quickly knocked on the door. Now in my cloudy mind, I was thinking I wonder if Ron knew that is Josh, especially when Ron said "who is it?" Now for as long as I have been married to him he always says, who is it? Like who the heck else would it be? So he asked Josh, who said, "It's me". Well as luck would have it I always would say, "It's me". I also know that Ron usually gets ready; well, free from any garment restrictions…I know, TMI, but it is important to get the full effect of what is about to happen.

So after Josh says, "it's me", Ron says, "Come in", and he opens the door, and in unison both my husband and my son start screaming like little girls. I look up to see Josh covering his eyes like they were burning in his head and Ron getting shaving cream everywhere. Well, I laughed until I cried. Ron and Josh were both trying to blame each other, then trying to blame me for this assault on their eyes and mind. Still makes me laugh every time I think about it. Thank you Lord for the everyday mishaps we have.

SCRIPTURE:

"Let all bitterness, and wrath, and anger, and clamour, and evil speaking, be put away from you, with all malice; And be ye kind one to another, tender hearted, forgiving one another, even as God for Christ's sake hath forgiven you." Ephesians 4:31-32 (KJV)

WORDS OF ENCOURAGEMENT FOR THE WEEK:

DAY ONE HUNDRED NINETY-FIVE – At this point in time you are outrageously funny, stupendously gifted, phenomenally insightful, and breathtakingly beautiful, but don't worry it's only Tuesday. Just wait, you'll get better!

DAY ONE HUNDRED NINETY-SIX – There is nothing wrong with taking a stand; but make sure it is not higher than your stand for Christ.

DAY ONE HUNDRED NINETY-SEVEN – Regardless of what you have heard on the news. In spite of what you have seen, even if you can't feel it, make no mistake, God is still in control. Matthew 24:6 (NIV) says, "You will hear of wars and rumors of wars, but see to it that you are not alarmed. Such things must happen, but the end is still to come." Jesus talked about this "panic" two thousand years ago. God's people need to find rest in knowing that He has a plan for us and this world.

DAY ONE HUNDRED NINETY-EIGHT – If you ever find your-self in Massachusetts you may want to understand a few choice words to help you in understanding the language barrier. Don't ask someone to say Pahk the cah in Hahvuhd yahd; this could result in some unpleasant remarks. Paw-tee is potty, and Paw-taa is Party. Down cella means in the basement. You will be brought hot tea if you just ask for tea. Wus-tah is Worcester and Bubbla is a water fountain. If you want ice cream and sprinkles ask for ice cream and jimmies. A Chowdahead is someone who doesn't have a clue. If someone is wicked awesome that means they are really good. We don't always pronounce the letter "r" in the right places, but don't worry we'll add them on to other words as needed. This may explain why I never did well in spelling bees.

DAY ONE HUNDRED NINETY-NINE – For every negative comment made, there will be words of affirmation in your defense. For every bite from the serpent, there is an antidote to take the sting away. God will speak redemption in to your life. He will heal the soul to restoration. Choosing God will always be the right answer.

DAY TWO HUNDRED – Have you ever driven down the highway and pulled off to get something to eat, only to be disappointed there is only one place in town? It looks old and worn out, besides there are a lot of motorcycles in the parking lot. You cautiously get out and make your way inside. The wallpaper is faded, and those seats have seen better days, but there's something friendly and familiar in there. We place our order, and with the first bite I know we have experienced something that few people outside of town ever have the privilege of eating. The type of meal that has been cooked the same way for generations, and it is heavenly. These types of restaurants remind me not be so judgmental when it comes to people. Some of us may look worn out and rough around the edges, but inside you will find some of the best love, joy, and laughter you'll ever experience. Side note: If you see a lot of motorcycles at a particular restaurant, stop and go inside, that usually means the food is awesome, and so are the riders.

DAY TWO HUNDRED-ONE – Words on the lips, written down on paper, or on the screen can excite us, make us cry, or give us encouragement. Words can open our imagination to other worlds. Words can give us hope to continue on and words can bring about our destiny. A simple word can stop us dead in our tracks and terrify us to move forward. Words can put a smile on our face or make us laugh out loud. Words can create or destroy. Words can be used to mold how a child thinks and feels about themselves for their entire life. I really can't think of anything else that holds such power. Words echo throughout the generations. What are the words you leave for the world today?

DAY TWO HUNDRED-TWO – Praying to God is not like going through the drive-thru at McDonalds. Place your order and expect immediate results. Our God is more like a five star restaurant. He wants you to come in, experience the dining and savor each course, which was prepared especially for you. He wants you to be pampered by the staff. He wants to give you the royal treatment. He wants to be your only guest at the table, and when it's time to pay, He wants to pick up the bill – paid in full.

Mind over Matter

My mother has lived with us since 1996, and has been a blessing in our lives. She doesn't believe in slowing down or giving up. She always has a plan. She is an artist and avid gardener. She believes that all the world issues could simply be solved if only people spent more time in their own gardens. She does not like taking medications or going to the doctor. She knows it is necessary but that doesn't mean she has to like it.

Recently, she had hurt her hand while she was on a ladder, stripping off wallpaper border, holding a quart size can of paint, and painting a beam in her bedroom. She told me she was going to take her time, but had it completely done in three days. Apparently, she had hurt her hand in the process. After nursing it for several days, it was no better so we made an appointment at the doctors. We went and had the x-rays done and now we were sitting in the doctor's office waiting for the results. The physician's assistant started off by saying that she did not break her hand, but that the arthritis was so severe that she was amazed she could even hold a glass without being in pain constantly. She told my mother that her gardening days were over. At this point I knew how my mother was going to react. My mother may be older but she has all her own opinions and will not hesitate to share them. "Well, I have been gardening since I was three years old with my father. It is my greatest joy in life." "Since I now know that my hand is not broken, I will resume all normal activities".

The physician's assistant tried to explain how bad her arthritis was and that she was no longer able…she never finished her sentence. My mother again stated that her father had passed away in his gardens doing what he loved and that she planned on doing the same. The appointment was now over, with my mother getting up to leave. I thanked her for her time and we left. My mother has never complained again about her hand hurting her, she said it is just mind over matter and that arthritis did not matter!

SCRIPTURE:

> "Older women like wise are to be reverent in their behavior, not malicious gossips nor enslaved to much wine, teaching what is good, so that they may encourage the young women to love their husbands, to love their children, to be sensitive, pure, workers at home, kind, being subject to their own husbands, so that the word of God will not be dishonored." Titus 2: 3-5 (NASB)

WORDS OF ENCOURAGEMENT FOR THE WEEK:

DAY TWO HUNDRED-THREE – Let today be the day you dream it, you visualize it, you speak it, and you own it. Do not listen to why you can't do it, but how you can accomplish it, not thinking small, but aiming high. Keep your eyes on the prize for God wants to bless you today. Keep it in prayer and post scripture to encourage your spirit.

DAY TWO HUNDRED-FOUR – I have a major crush on Friday. Why? Friday is always the life of the party, you just say the name and everyone cheers. Friday's know how to dress, how to talk, and no one say's five o'clock like Friday, it gives me goose bumps. I heard a rumor that Friday dated Thursday for a while, but there wasn't any real chemistry. Let's face it; Thursdays are sort of a goody two shoe type of day, no offense. Saturday is a better fit for Friday and the whole week knows it. Mondays are downright depressing and everyone knows that Tuesdays and Wednesdays are big kiss ups. Sundays work best alone, so there you go. No matter what day of the week I'm in, always know that Friday is on my mind.

DAY TWO HUNDRED-FIVE – If I have been praying for a particular situation and I have not seen any movement or answers yet I ask myself, why? Is it me? Do I have any sin in my life that I have not confessed to God? Have I put down the things of this world and taken up the message of the cross? Am I serving others while I wait? Am I still complaining about it? Could I bring my prayer to a deeper level by fasting too? Am I changing my mind set to be more like Christ? After doing a spiritual check, I need to continue on until my prayers are answered. He will give me the peace I need to wait on His timing.

DAY TWO HUNDRED-SIX – Guard my mouth today Lord, let me speak your words, your wisdom, and your love. Keep me far from the gossip, the anger, and the bitterness.

DAY TWO HUNDRED-SEVEN – God has given us four legged animals to love, to protect, and to add companionship to our lives. He sprinkled them with the same love He has for us. They love us unconditionally, they are always happy to see us, and if someone is trying to hurt us, watch out as they will protect us at any cost.

DAY TWO HUNDRED-EIGHT – Your words matter – think before you say. Your prayers matter – pray before you do. Your promises matter – stand firm before you pledge. Your relationships matter – prepare before you commit.

DAY TWO HUNDRED-NINE – My mother and I were waiting in line to pay for some roses, when the cashier said to me, "eleven dollars even". I hadn't planned on getting anything that day, so I did not bring my ATM or check book. I had exactly ten dollars to my name, so I asked my mother, "Can I borrow a dollar?" My mother gave me a dollar bill. Then the cashier rung up her order and it came to fifty-two dollars. She had exactly fifty-one dollars. She looked right at me and said, "Do you have a dollar?" Do you ever feel like you are experiencing déjà vu? I looked at her and said, "How could I have a dollar when I just asked you for a dollar?" We both got silly, laughing and realized we were the only ones laughing. The lady behind us gave my mom one dollar. We thanked her and laughed all the way to the car. Have you ever had an unexpected day? Has someone ever come to your rescue with no expectation of being compensated? Have you ever found the humor in your situation?

CHAPTER EIGHT
THE JOURNEY

Feed them, burp them, and put them to bed

Over the years Ron has been asked to serve in many different levels of church ministries. I remember one time when we were without a pastor for about four months. Our church was small and limited on funds so we only had enough to pay for visiting pastors on Sunday mornings only. Leaving the rest of the week up to the deacons, all four of them. Our congregation had about 140 parishioners.

It was a time of growth, a time of reflection, and on some weeks a time of wanting to choke some members down. I know that is not a very Christian attitude to have, but I developed a whole new respect for our pastors and their families. If I had to break it down, I would say the easy part was the physical labor: cleaning the church, mowing the lawn, visiting the sick in the hospital, even preparing the messages on Sunday and Wednesday nights, but by far the hardest part was the balancing of the congregation's many personality types. I mean the nitpicky, complaining, and the squabbles from some members. In all fairness, most of the congregation was pitching right in with us getting the jobs done around the church, but those pesky few in the church were enough to try any soul. I remember one

Thanksgiving we were interrupted by two families who had been arguing. Both continued to call Ron since he was the only one who could calm both sides down. After he got off the phone the last time, just before serving dessert, I said, "can't we just tar and feather them?" I couldn't help but relating to Job's wife just a bit. I know, not my finest hour as a deacon's wife, but some people can really suck the life right out of you.

I truly believe that every family should have to be a "pastor for the week" some time during the year to fully appreciate all they do. We need to be on our knees praying for our pastors every day for the devil is planning the downfall of the church as I type. We must be united, staying strong in Christ, loving and humble, always.

SCRIPTURE:

"Now we ask you brothers and sisters, to acknowledge those who work hard among you, who care for you in the Lord and admonish you. Hold them in the highest regard in love in peace among each other." 1 Thessalonians 5: 12, 13 (NIV)

WORDS OF ENCOURAGEMENT FOR THE WEEK:

DAY TWO HUNDRED-TEN – Come humbly, and He will exhort you up. Serve all, and He will build a kingdom. Stand up, and courage will fill you all the days of your life.

DAY TWO HUNDRED-ELEVEN – You can try to prepare in case of an emergency, but anyone who has lived long enough can tell you some events cannot even be imagined. When life's emergencies become overwhelming, lay your head on God's shoulder, put your hand in His, and give Him your heart to protect and love. Only He can get you through the most difficult storms.

DAY TWO HUNDRED TWELVE – No matter what kind of a day you've had, don't let your kids see anything but a loving parent. They are only little for a moment, protect them.

DAY TWO HUNDRED-THIRTEEN – You are going through an all consuming challenge right now. It's all you can think or talk about. This is a time you need to guard your emotions, and if you're not careful, they can bury you alive. You were never meant to handle your problems alone, to carry the guilt, and to walk a path of darkness with no light to carry you through. Your challenge can literally encase you in a self imposed prison. God wants you to know that He hears you, and if we have faith and trust in Him, He will restore you. He will give you peace and joy, even in the midst of the storm. He will heal the hurting heart, restore the broken body, and supply your daily needs. Start the new week a new year with an attitude of thankfulness for what you have, an attitude of not letting a situation dictate who you are, an attitude of victory.

DAY TWO HUNDRED-FOURTEEN – If I could go back in time, I would tell myself as a young mother that she needed to stop and play hide and seek more often. I would let her know she should cuddle her babies until they fell asleep. I would tell myself that housework would always be there, but her little ones won't be. I would gently whisper in her ear that she didn't have to be on so many committees. Before I would leave, I would kiss my babies oh so tenderly and tell them I loved them. My heart would ache until I came back through time to see my grandbabies waiting for me. God truly knows a mother's heart by giving her grandbabies to love and hold once more.

DAY TWO HUNDRED-FIFTEEN – A bad attitude, verbally expressed, is like passing on a highly contagious illness. It will stop the inspiration. It will blanket your entire family with gloom and doom. It will keep you up all night. No one will want to be around you. It will stop the flow of goodness and mercy, and you'll be in no mood to digest the spiritual word of God. Every negative comment will pass on to your family, your co-workers, and church. Everything you touch will become infected! Don't worry though, there is a cure. Stop complaining! Let the praise words flow from your mouth several times a day. Very soon kindness, mercy and love will get you back on your feet and on the path to spiritual wellness. Stay healthy my friends and remember you are loved today!

DAY TWO HUNDRED-SIXTEEN – God is my fortress, I will not be moved. I will not look to the left or to the right, but will keep my eyes centered on Him. The breakthrough is right around the corner and I will not be shaken. I am weak, but He is strong. I may have been knocked down, but I am not out. I have felt the pain, but will push through. I will take hold and not let loose, the battle is already won. God uses all things to glorify His kingdom.

The Anniversary Dinner

It was our twenty-sixth wedding anniversary and Ron wanted to take me somewhere nice and unexpected. Once we hit twenty years of marriage we try to do something "big" every five years. Of course the year after doing something grand can be something of a let-down the following year. Now, Ron and I are pretty average, never had a lot of money, but we enjoy each other's company and just going to a local restaurant is just fine with me. Still, Ron wanted to dazzle me. We got dressed up and headed to the French quarter in downtown Charleston. How exciting, a grown up restaurant, with no kids to embarrass us. We could take our time and just enjoy the grown up atmosphere.

We walked hand in hand to the restaurant at 5:00 p.m. and we were the first to arrive. The building was very old, brick and stone. This building had a rich history, with wood beams, and it was gorgeous to just sit and wonder what this old building had seen in its day. We were greeted by the hostess, who looked like a million bucks, and I suddenly felt under dressed. As she was seating us, she began to tell us about "our" chef and the "art" of preparing each meal, as well as what's involved, the cuts of meat, and the homegrown herbs and spices. We nodded and secretly didn't understand one word she just said. I was starting to feel a little bit like the Beverly Hillbillies again. I looked over at the wall of wine bottles, each one on a pedestal with a card explaining the glorious history of each wine and the owners. Wow, who knew? I guess any sophisticated person who would be eating at this restaurant.

They handed us the menu, which was all hand written in old English. I was just scanning for a word I understood, chicken or beef. The waiter approached us, asking if we would like a glass of wine. Not just any glass of wine, but wine from the finest grapes aged to perfection, and would we care to explore the wonderful world of wine tasting. I'm paraphrasing of course, but he was talking about those wines like he was dating them.

So Ron took charge, as the man, asking what kind of drinks they had that included cute pink umbrellas? Oh my goodness, you might have thought we slapped him in the face. "Sir, we do not carry a line of frozen drinks, especially the cute pink umbrella kind." Well, I guess he told us. May I add something that does irritate me, I don't like waiters who are snobbier than us, I immediately chimed in, "we will have two sweet teas". Our waiter looked one last time at the rows of delicious wines and went back to the kitchen. I really wanted the steak but it was forty dollars. Ron said I deserved it and a steak was what I was going have. I have to say the atmosphere and watching people walk by on the street was first rate. Ah, finally our sweet teas had arrived. The waiter, once again, telling us about the custom made teas the chef uses to prepare his drinks. Oh man, that tea tasted like I was drinking a bottle of perfume.

Ron was going to complain, but I begged him not to. After all, was it their fault our tongues were not delicate enough to understand the special herbs used to create this tea? We will suck it up and pretend we were wealthy and educated on such matters. The waiter brought us our bread and butter, which was awesome. I believe it was some type of locally grown multi grain bread. It was so good, just a little hard to break off. Luckily for me I have my own teeth so I just kept pulling and chewing until a piece came off. Ron asked the waiter if it was a slow night since we were the only ones there. I personally would not have asked any questions, since everything seemed to offend him. But the waiter told us that their diners usually strolled in around 8:00 p.m., more on the European time schedule, not like us, who were use to the early bird specials. I added the last part, because now I felt I was starting to be able to read his mind.

Finally, the meal comes, and I have to say, my steak was one of the best steaks I had ever eaten in my life. It was in some type of sauce which melted the steak in my mouth. But Ron, who wanted everything perfect for me, knowing that I loved A-1 steak sauce, asked the waiter if he could bring us a bottle. The look on our waiter's face was like this truly is the last straw, "Sir", he said, "this would be a great insult to the chef to pour this on to his creation." At this point I had to throw Ron under the bus, "no sir", I said, "this would be an insult to add A-1 steak sauce on to this perfectly custom made steak". The waiter gave Ron one final look before heading back into the kitchen. Pretty soon the chef came out from the back. Holy smoke, were they going to kick us out of the restaurant?

He was wicked awesome, a transplant from Massachusetts, been down here a few months and he had heard me talking. What a joy to talk to him and we complimented him on a superb dinner. It truly was the best steak dinner I had ever eaten. All in all we had a wonderful night out. I found out that we didn't need small children around us to be embarrassing, we did fine on our own. Even though we were ignorant on many subjects, we could still, after all these years, enjoy each other's company and enjoy the history of this beautiful city of Charleston. Life is too short to let a waiter spoil our night. We strolled hand in hand around the cobble stoned streets in this city rich in history and honor.

"Be diligent to present yourself approved to God, a worker who does not need to be ashamed, rightly dividing the world of truth." II Timothy 2:15 (NKJV)

WORDS OF ENCOURAGEMENT FOR THE WEEK:

DAY TWO HUNDRED-SEVENTEEN – I went out tonight with my old elementary school friends from Rutland. Some of us hadn't seen each other in thirty-five plus years. We laughed, we cried, we remembered, and we got yelled by another table to keep it down. Some things never change. Love my Rutland girls! I hope you are able to share your history with people who knew you when all you cared about was playing hide and seek and going to the town pool to see friends.

DAY TWO HUNDRED-EIGHTEEN – Do you suffer from a form of psychological abuse? Is there a loop in your mind of self doubt, guilt, fear, anxiety, or worry about the smallest details? Do you have endless questions that have no real answers? There is a negative force inside your mind. These negative forces' ONLY job is to confuse and torment you from doing what God has called you to do. The Bible tells us to set our minds on prayer and thanksgiving, praising Him in all things. At first it may be difficult, but I like to make a game of it. I love to win. So, every time I have such thoughts I set my mind to the positive and on the goodness of God's blessings. I will speak the blessings out loud which really helped keep me focused. It doesn't happen overnight, but you will have victory over your mind and peace will soon follow.

DAY TWO HUNDRED-NINETEEN – We came together on that early May morning to hear some women missionaries share their life experiences in other countries. We were finishing up brunch when I jokingly said to my table, "I'm glad they were called, because I could never do that." The first missionary, who stood up and started her speech by saying, "Never say you'll never become a missionary, if that is what God has planned for you to do." I was embarrassed and convicted all at once. It left such an impact that I have never forgotten those words. How many times have I said I cannot or will not do something just because I didn't feel qualified, for the task asked of me? Lord, use me, mold me, shape me, and send me to where your will is for my life. If God ordains you to do something or go somewhere, He will open doors. He will clear the streets, He will soften the hard hearts, and He will make sure you will succeed in all you do.

DAY TWO HUNDRED TWENTY – You fought hard, there were many casualties, you took no prisoners, but God says tell them about the love of Christ – who will listen now? Don't let something become so important that you forget the reason you are here, to share the gospel of Christ to a world that is lost.

DAY TWO HUNDRED TWENTY-ONE – I will not bring forth into today any ugliness from yesterday. For why would I want to poison a new day? Today has not been formed. There is no prejudice, and no evil has been committed – not yet. Gossip, hatred, and bitterness filled my day yesterday, but not today. There is still hope. Don't return anger with anger. Let the bitterness drop at your feet. Instead pick up one act of kindness. Let the difference between today and yesterday be your mind set. You can change. I believe in you and so does God.

DAY TWO HUNDRED TWENTY-TWO – "At the moment you hold your grandchild in your arms, you know it was worth the teen-age years of their parents." Author Unknown

DAY TWO HUNDRED TWENTY-THREE – Have you ever felt at times like you were walking a tight-rope across the Grand Canyon, only to get half way out and you suddenly realize you are all alone? There are some emergencies or unforeseen situations that can make us feel totally isolated, and so afraid we stop dead in our tracks. Many times this happens in the middle of the night, at least for me. During the day I have my prayer contacts, everything seems much clearer, but at night, there is no one to call but God. He is always on call. He always works the night shift. I was reminded of this last night during prayer, while all alone in the midst of a storm. He reminded me gently that He was in control, that I did not need anyone else. It was between Him and me. Thank you Father, for the times I can hear your voice so clearly.

A Thought
(portion of Pastor Larry Burgbacher sermon)

Imagine that you have access to the Great White Throne of God. You are a child of the King and He has given you the key to the room. The throne which is filled with angelic beings of every kind, where their only job is to glorify, praise, worship, bow down, and lift up the name of the Holy One, the Great I AM.

Now, you use your key, given only to His children. You turn the golden knob and enter. As you walk to the center of the room, all eyes are on you. The brightness of the throne is overwhelming, yet you can see. You are on a mission this morning to speak to your Heavenly Father. You walk to the bottom of His majestic throne.

He looks down, lovingly, puts His hand up to silence everyone in the room. His child has come to speak to Him and He doesn't want to miss a word. You have His full attention and you say, "God, let me have a good day." Then you proceed to walk out the same way you came in. He is our Holy Father. Speak to Him, for He deserves our praise and worship!

SCRIPTURE:

> "Whenever the living creatures give glory, honor, and thanks to him who sits on the throne, who lives forever and ever, the twenty-four elders fall down before him who sits on the throne and worship him who lives forever and ever. They lay their crowns before the throne and say, You, are worthy, our Lord and God, to receive glory and honor and power, for you created all things, and by your will they were created and have their being." Revelation 4: 9-11 (NIV)

WORDS OF ENCOURAGEMENT FOR THE WEEK:

DAY TWO HUNDRED TWENTY-FOUR – If you have known me any length of time, I'm sure I have disappointed you in some way. Thankfully, my friends and family love me anyway, but remember only God can be the perfect example on how to live a life that is pleasing to Him.

DAY TWO HUNDRED TWENTY-FIVE – Do you keep failing the same test? Next time, try a different way in preparing how you take your test. If the same problem keeps happening in your life, try something different – stay calm, don't react with your gut, but remember what you've studied, and tell yourself you've got this. Your teacher has prepared you to pass. Change the attitude and you'll pass with flying colors.

DAY TWO HUNDRED TWENTY-SIX – Highly recommend the book, *Battlefield of the Mind,* by Joyce Meyers. It changed my spiritual life.

DAY TWO HUNDRED TWENTY-SEVEN – Pick Your Poison: Stress, bitterness, hatred, non-forgiving, worry, anxiety, fear or guilt. Do you have any of these emotions running rampant in your mind? These poisons will lead to health issues, mental illness, and spiritual death. Make sure you put these in a locked cabinet with a sticker that has a cross bone and skull on it.

DAY TWO HUNDRED TWENTY-EIGHT – I am grateful for the day and all that life has to offer. Today, I wear my scars openly so that I will not become prideful. I will walk carefully so not to trample the garden. I will remember all that God has given me and be joyful, for life is precious.

DAY TWO HUNDRED TWENTY-NINE – Don't get caught up in the panic, don't say we're doomed – we have hope in Him. Hope in a Savior, hope for a better tomorrow. No matter what the world shows us, no matter what the reporters tell us, remember God has a plan, trust Him – we are going to be okay. If the world sees us yelling "the sky is falling", why would the world believe we serve an All Mighty God?

DAY TWO HUNDRED THIRTY – Prepare now for the battle is coming. For the time will come when you will need your wits about you, you will be tossed about, fear will grip your heart, but eventually the kids will come home from school and you better have after school snacks ready.

Random Life's Lessons

Life is not fair, so stop acting like the world owes you something. Bad things happen to good people, we are all on a life journey. Betrayal always hurts. Great marriages don't just happen. If you don't think your life turned out as you planned, change the plan. Giving 10% to God isn't about the money. If you're feeling hurt that no one ever invites you over to their house, then you should invite all those people who never get an invitation out to come to your house. God is not a dirty word, Holy is His name. I will not argue about politics, I will pray about my decision and pray for whoever gets in to office.

Surround yourself with positive people. No one's life is perfect, no matter what you see on the outside. Bitterness is a cancer to your spirit. Laughter gets all the toxins out and clears up your acne. Our senior citizens are a wealth of information; listen to them before it's too late. You don't know everything, so stop acting like you do. Grandchildren are as perfect as you can get this side of Heaven. If you have a job you're blessed, if you have a home you're blessed, and if you have family and friends, you're blessed. If you eat too much you'll get fat. If you don't like how someone is treating you – pray for them. It's ok to say "no".

SCRIPTURE:

> "Blessed be God, even the Father of our Lord Jesus Christ, the Father of mercies, and the God of all comfort; Who comforeth us in all our tribulation, that we may be able to comfort them which are in any trouble, by the comfort wherewith we ourselves are comforted of God." II Corinthians 1: 3-4 (KJV)

WORDS OF ENCOURAGEMENT FOR THE WEEK:

DAY TWO HUNDRED THIRTY-ONE – How do you fight the negative, the bitterness, and the hurt? Speak the positive, read the Word, sing His praises, and count your blessings. It begins with you and ends with God.

DAY TWO HUNDRED THIRTY-TWO – God doesn't care what kind of house you have, how well you dress, how skinny or fat you are, or what your political views are. He sees your heart. How is your relationship, your personal relationship, with Him?

DAY TWO HUNDRED THIRTY-THREE – Complaining attracts the dark side to you. It's like a magnet to your soul. The more you complain, the harder it is to break free. It not only affects you, but your entire household, workplace, and church. I am begging you to stop it immediately.

DAY TWO HUNDRED THIRTY-FOUR – "Being happy and having joy in your heart are two separate matters all together. Happiness depends on your circumstances, while joy is there regardless of your circumstances. Happiness is a feeling, while joy is the well being in your spirit". By Larry Burgbacher

DAY TWO HUNDRED THIRTY-FIVE – Not everyone is at your level – Remember you were there once too – love people where they are!

DAY TWO HUNDRED THIRTY-SIX – Many years ago, when I was a young mother, I found myself filled with stress and worry, I asked God, "Why"? I was pregnant with our fourth child and Ron had been laid off from work for months. We had bill collectors calling us. Ron had been on hundreds of job interviews. "Lord", I cried out, "where are you?" "We have been faithful, we are your children, where are our blessings?" I felt so alone and abandoned. With much bitterness and anger, I opened my Bible to read these verses in Matthew 8:26 (NIV), "He replied, you of little faith, why are you so afraid? Then He got up and rebuked the winds and waves, and it was completely calm." I took my eyes off of Him and looked only at the problem. Have you ever done this? He will calm the storms of your life, keep the faith.

DAY TWO HUNDRED THIRTY-SEVEN – Salvation is a GIFT from God, you can't earn it, suffer for it, or buy it...you can just accept it. Ask Jesus into your heart today, you'll never regret it!

CHAPTER NINE

THE LESSON

Watch your step

Please be advised: If you are sensitive to life's messier side, you may want to skip this story entirely. The day started simple enough. Ron was coming home at 10:00 a.m. and we were going to finish up with all our Christmas shopping. Yes, it was going to be an awesome day. After all, I had written about being thankful just that morning on my Facebook page.

Have you ever gone shopping with a two year old grand-daughter and a husband who would rather do anything else but shop? After hours of trying to keeping our little peanut enter-tained and wanting to just head home, I convinced my husband into just one more stop. I could see by Ron's face I had pushed the "envelope" to the limits. Ron was very ready to go home. So, I knew I must be quick like a bunny. I had my list, I knew where everything was, I saw an empty cart, and I was a woman on a mission. I took a few steps and started to slide. Catching myself I looked down to see if there was some water on the floor.

No water, not today. Today it was a pile of POOP! Not a dot of poop, not a little mud, but honest to goodness, it was like an entire family had pooped in a bag and they rushed it over to dump it onto the floor right next to the check-out. I swear it was still steaming. Are you kidding me? I wanted to cry, gag, scream, what to do, what to do? I looked for help since I was unable to move without furthering additional poop on me and making me fall. I looked, but no one would look at me, everyone who started to look, looked down and then made a face. I was a leper in my own community. So in my mother voice, nice and clear I yelled out, "EVERYONE PLEASE BE CAREFUL, I JUST STEPPED INTO A PILE OF POOP. I DON'T WANT ANYONE TO GET HURT, THERE IS A LOT HERE, SO PLEASE BE VERY CAREFUL OF THE POOP THAT SURROUNDS ME."

The store manager came over, "Can I help you?" she said. I pointed down. She said she'd get me some help, as I watched her trying to control her gagging reflex. Guess who she sends over? The ninety year old greeter! God love her, she was the only one who helped me. So, of course the entire time she was getting water to flush it away, orange cones and lots of paper towels. I continued on in my quest to save others from the fate I had, yelling, I AM STANDING IN A PILE OF POOP - PLEASE BE CAREFUL! Not one of my proudest moments, but necessary so others may be spared the same fate. Oh, and by the way, Ron saw me and continued walking on, but really, who could blame him? I was a mess, literally a mess!

I like to take away with each embarrassing moment a lesson to be learned. Even the best laid plans can be interrupted when poop happens. It may be humbling, it may be messy. It may be lonely, but you will get through it too.

SCRIPTURE:

"Though I walk in the midst of trouble, thou wilt revive me; thou shalt stretch forth thine hand against the wrath of mine enemies, and thy right hand shall save me." Psalm 138:7 (KJV)

WORDS OF ENCOURAGEMENT FOR THE WEEK:

DAY TWO HUNDRED THIRTY-EIGHT – You do realize that going to church is just the start off point, right? Going to church is not the final destination, but simply the place to fill up on spiritual fuel to go out and start your ministry. When you are no longer satisfied to just sit in the pew; take a step into the aisle, move on down to the altar, and watch what God can do with your life.

DAY TWO HUNDRED THIRTY-NINE – Praise Him
Thankful for second chances,
honored to be called,
Grateful for His grace and mercy,
humbled when I fall,
joyful in just the living,
inspired by the day,
encouraged by the friendships,
and loved along the way!

DAY TWO HUNDRED FORTY – Stop talking about all the things that could go wrong; you're going to talk yourself right out of your destiny!

DAY TWO HUNDRED FORTY-ONE – There will be times when someone will enter your life who are never happy or content. They truly believe if they only had a different job, a different church, new neighbors, bigger home or nicer family, only then could they be truly happy. There is no joy for them, or you. You will not be able to make them happy. This really has nothing to do with you. This has been a problem that has been festering for a long time. For your own peace of mind, you need to step back and distance yourself from them before you are sucked into the vortex of despair too. With that said, let me say, "no one is a lost cause". Prayer is the only avenue to take in these cases. God can release them from this bondage. God can deliver them from this torment and only God can bring them true joy.

DAY TWO HUNDRED FORTY-TWO – Listen, many of us carry an invisible ball and chain. The chain of bitterness, the chain of strife, the chain of hurt, the chain of hate, the chain of pride, the chain of debt, the chain of depression, the chain of not letting go, and the chain of unbelief – God can remove your chains. He will take each link off Himself and throw them into the deepest part of the sea. He will hear you today, push through.

DAY TWO HUNDRED FORTY-THREE – We have plenty of pew warmers. What we need is a hand, a set of feet, and a willing spirit to hand out meals to the homeless, to walk to a village to share the good news of Jesus Christ, and to not complain about your situation. We have plenty of buts, but not enough hearts.

DAY TWO HUNDRED FORTY-FOUR – It's a great day to speak to the King and receive His favor. It's a great day to instill in your children a lesson of hope and encouragement. It's a great day to go to the mountains or the sea and look at His majestic power. Each day you need to ask yourself what are you expecting in your life. Expect the best, expect the miracle, and expect that God knows what is best for you.

If it's not your problem

After eating out for breakfast, Jenni, Bridget and I (because you know girls go to the bathroom in packs) went to the restroom. While I was waiting my turn, I could hear that Jenni was having a somewhat difficult time opening the stall door. She sounded a little panicked that she could not get it opened. Fortunately, I was there to calm her down and I told her to simply keep turning the knob slowly, and within thirty seconds she was free. When it was my turn I noticed how easy it was to lock and I had to chuckle at how silly people get when they can't get out of a tight situation.

When I went to open the door, I noticed that every time I turned the knob it would freeze up. Okay, I said to myself, I'll just try turning the knob slowly, nope, nothing. I started to gently shake the door, nope. I started to knock on the door telling Bridget and Jenni that I was stuck, no answer. I grabbed the locked door and started shaking it more violently. Now I'm looking for another way out, there was maybe an eight inch opening in the bottom and top of the door, no that way would not be possible either. Now I am speaking loudly for help, but there was no response, I could feel my heart beginning to race and it was getting really hot in there.

After what seemed like an eternity, four minutes, I was free, and I stumbled out. I went outside to see the girls chatting away. Jenni said, "What took you so long?" I said, "I got stuck and no one helped me". Jenni looked at me and said, "Did you turn the knob slowly?" The lesson: It is always easy when you're not the one going through it!

SCRIPTURE:

"My brethren, count it all joy when you fall into various trials, knowing that the testing of your faith produces patience. But let patience have its perfect work, that you may be perfect and complete, lacking nothing." James 1:2-4 (NKJV)

WORDS OF ENCOURAGEMENT FOR THE WEEK:

DAY TWO HUNDRED FORTY-FIVE – Keep believing, keep the faith, keep hoping, keep looking for the good in others, keep loving, keep the commandments, keep praying, and keep your eyes on God and Him alone. KEEP – to bring something closer to yourself, not letting go.

DAY TWO HUNDRED FORTY-SIX – It is okay to say NO. Don't let someone make you feel inadequate, or say you are backslid, simply because you want to either step down from a position, or not take another ministry on to an already busy schedule. With that said, I would like to strongly encourage you to do something! If you feel "burnt" out doing one thing, look around. I'm sure there are other places to serve at church. Look at your spiritual gifts and pray about where God would like to see you serving.

DAY TWO HUNDRED FORTY-SEVEN – Valentine's Day is a great day to give someone your heart – God. What a tremendous day to share a meal with someone who is hungry – the homeless. It's a superb day to send flowers – to the widow. How awesome would it be to say I love you – to the child. It's a splendid day to send a card – to the lonely. Let today be the day you are someone else's Valentine.

DAY TWO HUNDRED FORTY-EIGHT – In the end, hope is all we have. In the middle we have a journey to complete. In the beginning we found our faith.

DAY TWO HUNDRED FORTY-NINE – The answered prayer, how sweet the sound. I love watching it unfold, and I love when my spirit suddenly realizes it is happening before my eyes. I love the overwhelming peace and joy that fills up inside me - feeling like it is going to escape through my fingertips. I love how I can hear His voice, "I heard you all along".

DAY TWO HUNDRED FIFTY – Until you make it right with your heavenly Father, nothing will fall into place for you. Too harsh? It will be your saving grace.

DAY TWO HUNDRED FIFTY-ONE – <u>Nana moment:</u> Ron and I were spending some quality time with our grandchild recently. The hotel we had chosen seemed to only have seniors registered, but as long as the hotel had a pool that was okay with him. He was only about four years old and was having such a wonderful time when it hit me that it had been a while since I had taken him to the potty. Trying to be a responsible adult, I told him to "come out and let's go potty". He yelled back, "It's okay Nana, I already went in the pool". I looked over at some of the people sitting close by and they were making faces of disgust. Some people are so judgmental. I looked at them and said, "Like you never have," then grabbed my little one and hurried along, before a mob formed.

Football season

As many of you know, football season has started, so Ron has been watching his fair share while I look at pictures of the grandkids on Facebook or read from my kindle. Every once in a while I look and watch for a minute or two and a thought crosses my mind. We are like quarterbacks (that's the guy who runs with the ball, right?) and the opposing team reminds me of those negative forces, trying to push us down every chance they get. The coach reminds me of God, everyone gets their orders from him. The coach never takes his eyes off the ball, the prize. He tells the quarterback, "Do what you need to do to be successful and get over to the goal posts", our destination to greatness. It's not easy, seems like every time I check he is getting tackled and all he gets is a few feet further.

We are not alone though, the rest of the team is there too, and their job is to protect the quarterback, us. Now these guys remind me of our intercessory prayer friends, and even angels, blocking the evil forces from getting to us. It must seem pretty dark when that quarterback gets tackled and everyone on the opposing team is on top of him, but he doesn't give up. He may need to change the plan around, but eventually he gets an opening and he runs. He runs like he is on fire, he runs with one goal in mind, to get through the goal posts and make that touchdown. When he does, he falls to his knees in appreciation, the team goes crazy, the crowd cheers him on, and the coach beams with pride, it was a team effort, and we win the game.

The lesson – when you are thrown into the game, you don't go alone. God equips you with an entire team of players and He will never take His eyes off of you. The saints from heaven believe in you and will cheer you on to the finish line. Believe in yourself, you can do this.

"Fight the good fight of the faith. Take hold of the eternal life to which you were called when you made your good confession in the presence of many witnesses." I Timothy 6:12 (NIV)

WORDS OF ENCOURAGEMENT FOR THE WEEK:

DAY TWO HUNDRED FIFTY-TWO – When going on vacation, I enjoy every part of the planning process. I am a planner, so I am really in my element. We discuss, we save, and we invite others to join us. I love the details, but there are some things I simply cannot plan for. I cannot control the weather. I cannot control a potential accident. I am trusting, the pilot and or the captain of the ship to get us safely to our destination. If I worried about every part of the trip it would start to take all the fun out of it. I will not lose sleep over something I simply have no control over. As I know from personal experience, my vacations have a way of taking on a life of their own, but they do make a fun story that I can share with family and friends. Learn to love the unexpected, ready or not here it comes.

DAY TWO HUNDRED FIFTY-THREE – A few years ago Ron and I were having a disagreement. I, of course, was winning. I made all my points, then looked over smugly at my husband, who is a humble man. All he said were two words, "let's pray". Guess who won? How did that happen? I was wrong on two points. First point, I was too angry to pray, and that alone let me know that my spirit was not right. Secondly, I wanted to gloat. I could not pray and have the spirit of pride in me at the same time. Fight fair in a relationship. A good indication to know if you are right or not is to be willing to pray and let the spirit guide you.

DAY TWO HUNDRED FIFTY-FOUR – What is your life story saying about you? What would the title of your movie be called? *Gone With the Wind? It's a Wonderful Life? Facing the Giants? Patton?* How about *Star Wars?* Would it be a comedy or a tragedy? Would anyone want to see your movie? Would you want to see your movie? You are the writer, director and actor in your movie - make it an Oscar worthy production.

DAY TWO HUNDRED FIFTY-FIVE – I have noticed, as a society, that we still have a "mob" mentality; this seems especially evident after a tragedy and when the "villain" kills themselves. The news media is so eager to point the finger that they can leave a trail of destruction behind. They will blame the family of the villain. They will blame the teachers, the doctors, the roommates, the neighbors, even the family dog. They will go to any measure to bring out the worst parts of people's lives just in time for the six o'clock news and we can't get enough. Stand out and stop thinking like a mob. Next time pray for all the victims in a senseless act.

DAY TWO HUNDRED FIFTY-SIX – Embarrassed, humbled, and honored to say I just completed reading the entire Bible in one year. After all these years as a Christian, I just never did it. Someone gave me the NIV Daily Bible and I decided this was the year to do it. I had no idea I was missing the best part – a one on one conversation with my heavenly Father. Make a new start and begin reading today, you'll be profoundly surprised.

DAY TWO HUNDRED FIFTY-SEVEN – Today is not a day to stress, but to impress. Today is not a day to worry, but to serve. Today is not a day to complain, but to praise. Today you get to choose, will it be stress, worry, and complain, or impress, serve, and praise?

DAY TWO HUNDRED FIFTY-EIGHT – I suffered for years with my stress and worry. I used to tell people it was one of my "gifts". That was actually me being prideful – a state of constant confusion. I needed to confess my sin, humble myself, and share my worries to God, realizing He is in control. I needed a reality check, giving my mind the freedom to actually use my true spiritual gifts.

What's the number again?

I had set that Tuesday aside for deep cleaning my house. I pulled out my favorite jogging pants, with the holes in the knees, and one of Ron's old tee shirts that I believe I put on inside out, but I didn't care because I was on a cleaning mission. Right before I was to begin my major cleaning, my mother came upstairs and asked me if I could take her to get her three month hair perm. Sounds easy, right? I dropped her off and started the task of taking down curtains and cleaning baseboards, oh the smell of bleach filling my nostrils.

Just in the middle, I got a phone call that my mother was ready to be picked up. As I picked her up, she was wearing her scarf, I remember thinking the two of us looked like quite a pair.

I smelled like bleach and she smelled like a fresh perm. "Susie, could we stop by the dollar store?" I looked quickly in the car mirror and thought yikes, but we'll be quick, no one will ever see us. Of course I couldn't just go in to the dollar store and not pick up something. My mother was first, and as she waited for me, I saw her drifting over to look at something. My order came to $7.59. I went to use my ATM card, put my number in and the cashier said, "DENIED"!

We had been given new cards and new security numbers. Now what number was I suppose to put in again? After 3 failed attempts, the cashier, who by this time was irritated with me, said, "Do you have another way to pay?" I said, "Well, just use it as a credit card," big sigh from the cashier, "no ma'am, we don't take Master Card credit". Oh for Pete sake, so then I'm like, "I have plenty of money in my account." Oh my word, now I'm the poor lady who claims to have plenty of money but really doesn't. Looking for my mother, who always has some cash on her, now she looks like she just got off the boat herself with that scarf around her head, I'm yelling, "Mom, can I have some money?"

She is slightly hard of hearing so I had to repeat three times. As she walked closer to me she was yelling, "What's the matter Susie, you don't have any money?" "Mom, I have plenty of money, but my ATM card won't work, so can I borrow some money and I'll pay you back." The line is now seven deep and no one is looking very happy, nope, no support there. The entire time my mother was looking for exact change, she was also scolding me for using those new fangled ATM cards.

Lesson learned: Always assume someone will see you in public and always have a couple ways to pay for your purchases.

"The Lord sends poverty and wealth; he humbles and he exalts." 1 Samuel 2:7 (NIV)

WORDS OF ENCOURAGEMENT FOR THE WEEK:

DAY TWO HUNDRED FIFTY-NINE – The season of winter can be some of the most difficult times of our lives. The road is often long, dark, and uncertain. Make no mistake, He stands by your side, He does hear your cries, and He will feel your pain. Winter season can numb us into believing He is gone, but this is not true. God promises never to leave or forsake us.

DAY TWO HUNDRED SIXTY – "RENT TO OWN" – you are the landlord to your mind. Who will your tenants be? Do you want the one who is dirty, argumentative, and always late with the rent or the one who keeps the yard and house clean and they pay their rent right on time? You are the boss. You own the place. Take charge of your mind today.

DAY TWO HUNDRED SIXTY-ONE – Our lives are but a vapor, a blink, a moment in eternity. Make the moments count.

DAY TWO HUNDRED SIXTY-TWO – When I can't make sense or understand why a tragedy happens to good people, I find comfort in God's Word. "The Lord is my shepherd; I shall not want, He maketh me to lie down in green pastures; he leadeth me beside the still waters. He restoreth my soul; he leadeth me in the path of righteousness for his name's sake. Yea, though I walk through the valley of the shadow of death, I will fear no evil; for thou art with me; thy rod and thy staff comfort me". Psalm 23:1-4 (KJV)

DAY TWO HUNDRED SIXTY-THREE – It's not how well you are loved by your inner circle, but how well you can love others outside your comfort zone.

DAY TWO HUNDRED SIXTY-FOUR – If you've been praying for it, don't act so surprised when He answers you – It's insulting!

DAY TWO HUNDRED SIXTY-FIVE – Thank God He doesn't judge us like we judge others.

What are you wearing?

There we were, on our anniversary cruise, enjoying ourselves so much until I realized I had gotten a little too much sun. So, after a few hours pool side, I decided to take myself down to my cabin and finish enjoying my new kindle Ron had given me for our anniversary. It was the same cruise line we were on with our church friends. I had almost forgotten how much I loved to read. This new kindle was giving me the freedom to read anywhere and now I was back in my room, just enjoying the quiet, restful time on my bed.

Ron came in from the pool about an hour after me. He was just like a newspaper, filling me in on what our friends were doing. I don't know about you, but when I'm reading I'm not really paying too much attention to what is going on around me. I know, I'm kind of like a guy that way. Anyway, I heard Ron talking, as he was changing his swimwear. He was discussing tonight's planned activities. Our middle aged, white male, church friends were going to enter the Michael Jackson thriller dance competition. Let's face it; we had to stay up to watch that. He did have a point. That was going to be too juicy to pass up. Anyway, I heard Ron say he was going back on deck to watch the ping pong competition and he would be back in a while to get ready for dinner.

He asked me one more time if I wanted to go watch (Umm, no offense, but kill me). No, I did not want to watch the ping pong competition. Not when I had my new kindle to keep me company. I told him to go and have fun. Now, this was the first time I had really stopped to look up and see Ron. I noticed he was wearing his "old man" fishing hat. His nose had a little too much sunscreen on. He was sporting a bright canary yellow fruit of the loom tee-shirt, his underwear, and his hush puppy sandals. As I watched Ron turn and open the cabin door, I was conflicted. Should I miss the opportunity to laugh or should I save my husband from certain embarrassment? Ten years ago I may have let him go, but now, now I was back in church. "Ron," I said reluctantly, as he held the cabin door open. "What is it?" he replied, a little irritated that he needed to get to his fascinating ping pong game. "Ron, you, you, you, may," I stuttered, "you may want to look in the mirror before you leave".

I could see Ron was rolling his eyes, ever so slightly, as he moved to the right to get a final glimpse. "Oh dear lord, I am only wearing my underpants". As he shuts the cabin door quickly he looks at me in unbelief. "You were going to let me leave in my underwear, with our church friends around every corner?" I had to give one final smile at the mere thought of what could have been.

I know what you're thinking, poor Ron, I'd have to agree. What can I say "I'm a work in progress, right"? Lesson learned

– always look in the mirror before leaving your house, your room, or even your bathroom.

SCRIPTURE:

"with all humility and gentleness, with patience, showing tolerance for one another in love". Ephesians 4:2 (NASB)

WORDS OF ENCOURAGEMENT FOR THE WEEK:

DAY TWO HUNDRED SIXTY-SIX – Don't look at some Christians and reject Christ based on their actions. If you're looking for answers, look to God. He accepts you as you are. Don't let pride or past hurts stop you. He wants to have a personal relationship with you.

DAY TWO HUNDRED SIXTY-SEVEN – I needed to hear praise and worship today. It covers my soul like a warm, quilted blanket, an abundant spring of water for my thirsty bones, a cool cloth to my fevered brow. Being held in the arms of my Lord and Savior, sometimes no one can comfort me, but God Himself.

DAY TWO HUNDRED SIXTY-EIGHT – Nana moment: When Jake was five years old, we were driving down the highway in Sacramento. He seemed to be afraid every time we went through the underpass. As we started to approach one, I could see he was starting to tense up, so I told him, "wait for it", "wait for it", "wait for it", and as we went through we screamed as loud as we could. Guess what? He wasn't afraid anymore. We just laughed and laughed. I was so happy I could help. Jason, Jake's daddy, gave me a call about a week later. Apparently, they were driving down the California highway together when Jake said, "wait for it", "wait for it", "wait for it" and then screamed his head off while going through the underpass. Jason continued, "Mom, I have to give you an F minus". In all fairness, looking back, I can see that wasn't one of my better thought out plans.

DAY TWO HUNDRED SIXTY-NINE – Where was your moment? What defines you? Who are you? Why are you here? When will you know? Who will you listen to? When is it your turn? I know someone who has all the answers to your questions – our Heavenly Father!

DAY TWO HUNDRED SEVENTY – Without the Vine, I, the branch, would wither and die. The Vine has taken my iniquities and replaced it with virtuousness. The Vine is my redeemer, and I will hold on, all the days of my life.

DAY TWO HUNDRED SEVENTY-ONE – What is your spiritual gift? What do you gravitate to? What comes easily for you? The devil wants us to believe we have no gifts, especially if you compare yourself to someone on television or the pulpit on Sunday morning. In naming just a few spiritual gifts: Service, Discernment, Healing, Encouragement, Giving, Leadership, and Mercy, are just a few of the many God has given us. I have found it interesting that in many cases people will seek out in the job market the very jobs that match their spiritual gifts. Example: Someone who has the gift of healing and service may go in to the medical field. Someone who has the gift of leadership or encouragement will go in to the educational field. There are many great books out there on how to recognize your spiritual gifts, but don't over analyze or worry about it. Sometimes we start out with one or two, but as we grow in the Lord we can end up with several. Just know that God has made you unique, with your own set of gifts. Ask Him to open your eyes to what they are.

DAY TWO HUNDRED SEVENTY-TWO – God knows all about human nature – if every day was perfect why strive to the next level of greatness? People are usually very comfortable living inside their boxes, so sometimes God has to turn the box upside down, letting you fall. This may sound cruel to you, but no crueler than a mother bird kicking her babies out of the nest, how will they learn to fly otherwise? Finally this is the point in time when you see a glimpse of where you need to be and start walking the path to your destiny.

CHAPTER TEN

UNEXPLAINED EVENTS

Turn around

I was so irritated that September Sunday morning. I don't know
how many times I have told my family that I do not like being
late, being on time is being late to me. My daughter and grand-
daughter had spent the night on Saturday. Before going to bed,
I mentioned again about leaving the house by 8:30 a.m. to be on
time for the early service at 9:00 a.m. So, imagine my frustration
when I came downstairs to see my daughter with a towel still
around her head at 8:30 a.m. As I looked over at the clock, my
husband jumped up to hand the car keys, telling me to go ahead
and they would be along shortly.

I took the keys, mumbled something, and went out. We had
been on vacation for two weeks and I was really missing our
home church of praise and worship. Now, I was in no mood to
praise or worship. Side note: Do you ever start your Sunday's
on the wrong foot? I hope you know it's just the devil trying to
"steal" your joy away from worshipping God. I decided to take a
back road to church to try and save some time. As I turned the
corner, walking next to the road, I saw a young mother carrying two plastic bags and smoking a cigarette. Her little son was
crying and trying to keep up with her. I also noticed they were

barefoot and very dirty looking. The ground was very rocky and uneven. Nothing snaps you back into reality than seeing something outside your comfort zone.

I wondered where they could possibly be walking to? There were no housing developments in that direction. At that moment, I heard a voice inside my mind telling me to turn around and pick them up. I'm sure I didn't hear the voice correctly. I had to get to church. The voice came back at me, saying this time, "Are you kidding me?" So, I now tried to reason with this voice inside my head - you know I don't pick up hitch hikers. My dad had been attacked by a hitch hiker back in the 60's. I can't help them. I don't know what to do!

The voice was not sympathetic. The voice was also on a time schedule. The voice was clearly telling me to turn my car around and pick them up! If only I could be sure this is from God and not the devil. At that moment the voice increased the volume in my mind. Three times it said, "TURN AROUND, TURN AROUND, TURN AROUND!" What could I do? I turned around.

You see, if that woman had been alone, I would not have picked her up. If I had my family with me, I would not have stopped. But now I had the car seat available for that little boy. If I had been early, I wouldn't have taken the back road to try to cut off some time. I wasn't sure how I was going to help them, but my only job was to pick them up. The young mother had run away with her four year old son, because her husband was physically abusing them. I could see the bruises. She lived in Mount Pleasant and had no idea where she had parked her car. She was actually ten miles away from where I first picked them up. I believe God directed me in finding her car. She had parked down a deserted road which could not be seen from the main road. We (and by we, I mean I enlisted some pretty awesome friends who directed me to the right places) were able to get her into a shelter for abused families. We were able to get her car fixed, fill her gas tank, feed them, and clean them up. I had two other friends who said they had just passed that way too. One said she did not see a little boy, and the other one said she didn't see anyone.

I don't know why we all saw something different. I just knew I had to pick them up. I was humbled, I was shaking, and I was joyful all at the same time. To be able to help someone is truly what it's all about. That's why we go to church, to get out in our communities, and help those in need. Open your heart to the broken. Listen to the voice within your soul. I never heard from them again. Some said I was being used. Maybe so, but I know for sure I was suppose to pick them up. I was able to share the love of Christ and my spirit is at peace. I don't have to know the plans of God to trust Him.

SCRIPTURE:

"Do not forget to show hospitality to strangers, for by so doing some people have shown hospitality to angels without knowing it." Hebrews 13:2. (NIV).

WORDS OF ENCOURAGEMENT FOR THE WEEK:

DAY TWO HUNDRED SEVENTY-THREE – Dear Lord, I need you every hour, every minute of the day. The darkness threatens to overtake me, still I know, just one word, one look, one touch, and I will be healed.

DAY TWO HUNDRED SEVENTY-FOUR – Today I choose life. I choose to fight against the negative, the depressing, and the evil whispers. I am a child of God and I will overcome. I will finish what I have started. I will take His hand and He will fill me with His peace, His joy, and His love.

DAY TWO HUNDRED SEVENTY-FIVE – What can the body of Christ do for you? What I had forgotten was how much I had missed hearing the Word of God every week. What I had forgotten were the prayers the saints said over me. What I had forgotten was the rush of the Holy Spirit as He embraced me. What I had forgotten were the sweet sounds of praise and worship from the masses. What I had forgotten was how much He loved me. If you are not attending a Bible believing church, I encourage you to seek and find a place to share your faith with others. Church is not the perfect place with perfect people. We all make mistakes, but by God's grace we will pick ourselves up and try again, realizing we are not alone anymore.

DAY TWO HUNDRED SEVENTY-SIX – There comes a time in everyone's life where there will be a season of pain and heartache. When life gives someone you love a terrible blow and there are no words to comfort them. Some losses are so great that only God can penetrate that deep into the heart – hold them, love them, pray for them, and then let God comfort them in a way we will never be able to understand.

DAY TWO HUNDRED SEVENTY-SEVEN – I will forgive and move on. I will purge bitterness, hurt, and anger and move on. I will leave yesterday behind and move on. I will choose something better and move on. I will remove myself from the drama and move on. I will seek His will for my life and move on. I will take up the cross and move on. Moving On is the only way to cross the finish line strong!

DAY TWO HUNDRED SEVENTY-EIGHT – For those who live in Glory
Grateful I rise humbly I bow,
inspired to create, and loved by you all.
Admired your abilities,
strengthened by your words,
encouraged by the healing,
and marvel at what I've heard.
Redeemed I will follow,
courage I will find,
the masterpiece is now finished,
can glory be far behind?
Rest gently now my beloved
for soon all will be known,
the journey is now over,
and it's time to move on home.

DAY TWO HUNDRED SEVENTY-NINE – Be on your guard: The devil may even use your friends and family to persuade you against God's mission for your life. We all must be very careful to stay the course. Listen to God's voice. He has a plan for your life. If it's from God, it won't go away.

Wake up

When my daughter Jenni was 15 years old, we had many conversations about not burning candles in her room. Jenni assured me it was just for decoration and she would not be burning any of them in her room. Oh those famous last words from a teenager. The next morning, on a Saturday, I heard my mother's voice calling me. I had worked the night before and was hoping to sleep in until at least 9:00 a.m., but no, she was calling me with such urgency.

I was in no mood to get up yet and my mother yelled up once again, "SUSIE, WAKE UP NOW!" Oh for goodness sake, what did she want that was so urgent? I jumped out of bed and stomped my feet all the way downstairs, yelling downstairs, "What is it?" No answer. So, now I'm just irritated. I quickly went from room to room looking for my mother. I looked outside to see their car was gone. What is going on? Then, for some reason, that I can't explain, I went to Jenni's room. I knocked, she didn't answer. I opened the door to find the room was engulfed with black smoke.

I got Jenni up and out of her room, and opened the window. Her walls had a grayish look to them. Her rug was going to need a few cleanings from the black soot. Then I saw where the candle had been burning. The candle had long since burned out. But there was still a very small flame and the candle holder was black inside and very hot. We came so close to having a fire and Jenni could have inhaled all that black smoke. I went downstairs, shaken up by the events, and noticed a scrap of paper. My parents had written me a quick note as they had left early that morning to hit the spring sales at Home Depot and Lowes, so they would be gone all morning.

My parents had been gone a good hour before I ever heard the voice. Was it a mother's intuition, or an angel that called my name? Either way, beyond a shadow of a doubt, God's hand was in it.

"Are they not all ministering spirits, sent forth to minister for them who shall be heirs of salvation?" Hebrews 1:14 (KJV)

WORDS OF ENCOURAGEMENT FOR THE WEEK:

DAY TWO HUNDRED EIGHTY – As a parent we have the ability to know if our kids are happy, stressed out, or sick, just by the way they say "hi". Many of us even have the spiritual gift to sense if they are in physical danger or just going through a difficult period without them saying a word. This is a time for us, as parents/grandparents to keep them in constant prayer. As much as we love our children, our Heavenly Father loves them even more. Turn it over to Him, He will direct their paths, change the attitude, and protect them as He sees fit. After all, God is the supreme parent to us all.

DAY TWO HUNDRED EIGHTY-ONE – God can heal the soul, restore the body, and soothe the mind.

DAY TWO HUNDRED EIGHTY-TWO – What is your essence? Who are you? Not your physical being, not who you show to the world, or even your family. What is your essence? Not what you own or who you know. Strip away the physical, even how you think. What is your essence? Your essence is what God sees – it is the beauty of spirit. The flaws of never doing what we were destined to do. The heartache of choosing wrong, or the pain that is raw and indescribable. The potential of greatness that is inside of you! Here I am Lord. Let my essence be an extension – the hope of all things inspired by you.

DAY TWO HUNDRED EIGHTY-THREE – Don't let death catch you by surprise – know where you stand with eternity.

DAY TWO HUNDRED EIGHTY-FOUR – Humbly
Humbly I come,
humbly I bow,
humbly I speak
have I been called?
What will it take?
How will I know?
Is that His voice?
Have I been called?
He takes my hand gently,
together we move,
forever I am
I have been called!

DAY TWO HUNDRED EIGHTY-FIVE – Next time you are conflicted between telling your enemies off or showing them kindness – tell yourself I LOVE GOD more than I hate them. Sometimes it is that basic.

DAY TWO HUNDRED EIGHTY-SIX – Is your life a maze or are you on a journey? What's the difference? A maze was made especially to confuse and frustrate you, while a journey is made to develop you into the person you were meant to become. One leads nowhere, while the other one will bring you to the doorstep of your destiny.

Intercessory Prayers

For those of you that may be going through a challenge in your life and you are wondering if God hears you. We had been going through some trials which had kept us on our knees. I had a few of my intercessory prayer warriors joining me to pray.

Some weeks had passed and I did receive some emails and phone calls, telling me that God had laid us on their hearts to continue in prayer for us. Yet, in all fairness, these women of God had some inkling to what was going on, so I could see why they would want to follow up. It is so humbling, yet so powerful, to have someone pray for us.

On that following Friday, Ron came home from work and he said that the strangest thing happened to him today. He said he had received an email from someone he had worked with over twenty-five years ago. The man said he had tracked Ron down because for the past few weeks he had been waking up at 4:00 a.m. every morning with us on his mind. He was writing Ron to see if everyone was okay. Ron feeling embarrassed said everything was going good and he hoped everything was fine with him too. He immediately received another email back, "Listen, if God has been waking me up at 4:00 a.m. with you popping into my head, I want to know how to pray for you." He also had to do some detective work in locating Ron, since we had lost contact with him years earlier.

Now, you may be asking, why God would do this? I am not a spiritual expert, but I believe God uses people in the grand scheme of life. This way no one person can say it is because of their prayers it came to pass. God is so multi-layered, He was showing us that He was in control, He heard our prayers, He saw our situation, and He was increasing faith in many lives. Confirmation is a mighty testimony indeed.

"Again, truly I tell you that if two of you on earth agree about anything they ask for, it will be done for them by my Father in heaven. For where two or three gather in my name, there am I with them." Matthew 18: 19-20 (NIV)

WORDS OF ENCOURAGEMENT FOR THE WEEK:

DAY TWO HUNDRED EIGHTY-SEVEN – There are times, when all I can do is to look up to the heavens. When I am unable to understand the unthinkable, I look up. When those I love are hurt by evil and evil seems to be winning, I look up. My soul looks up because nothing compares to God. He is the maker of heaven and earth. He is the same God of yesterday, today and tomorrow. Our God is alive and He is watching. He has a plan and He knows what needs to be done. He has final say. He will bring justice to a corrupt world. Know this my friend, God sees all, knows all, and will do all in His perfect timing, not ours. Keep the faith my friend, these are the times that challenge our souls, but God's hands are on His children.

DAY TWO HUNDRED EIGHTY-EIGHT – So here I sit, on the couch, doing absolutely nothing! Two of my worst traits are being still and waiting! This was the week I had all planned out. I was going to get all my last minute holiday errands accomplished. So, what am I doing here? Fighting bronchitis and not doing much else. So, is God trying to show me something? Each time of reflection requires silence from me, and listening to His voice. So I will listen and wait for Him to remove the thorn from my side.

DAY TWO HUNDRED EIGHTY-NINE – Everyone wants the blessings, but no one wants to do the work. Everyone wants God to speak to them, but no one wants to listen. Everyone wants the peace, but no one wants to stop complaining. Everyone wants the joy, but no one wants to let go of the problem. Everyone wants a breakthrough, but no one wants to breakout. Let Him know you're ready now.

DAY TWO HUNDRED NINETY – No matter your age, if God has placed a dream inside of you, He will bring it about. He will give you the words, He will open the doors and He will release the knowledge necessary for you to get the task done. What must you do? Keep believing, keep praising, keep expecting, and don't give up. It took King David years of hiding in caves and fearing for his life before God placed him on the throne. God was preparing him to be a king. We are all on a life journey. Seek His face, His voice, and His will for your life!

DAY TWO HUNDRED NINETY-ONE – Many years ago we started attending a church where one particular lady did not like my accent. She especially did not like the way I said her name. I could tell I just grated on her nerves. In my defense, I tried very hard to say it correctly. But there was the letter "r" involved with her name, and well, it was not easy. I ended up sounding like I was coughing up a hair ball...no offense. She would usually "call me out", when there was a group of people around, on the proper usage of the English language. One particular Sunday morning I confessed my difficulty in saying her name, and decided I would call her something else. But much to her chagrin, I started calling her Frances, and I said it loud and proud. For some reason

I had no difficulty saying that name. Problem solved! I don't think she liked that either, but at least she didn't call me out on it anymore.

DAY TWO HUNDRED NINETY-TWO – Looking down the row of four ladies and two men getting pedicures on that particular afternoon, I have to say there are some pretty nasty feet out there. There are corns, bunions, dirty, cracked, and smelly feet. This gives a whole new meaning to "come as you are". It started me thinking how Jesus washed the feet of His disciples. You know those disciples feet went through some pretty gnarly things. Yet Jesus, the King of kings, washed their feet. Jesus is the epitome of a servant's heart. Can we do no less? Serve, as Christ served, let us humble ourselves to wash the feet of the world.

DAY TWO HUNDRED NINETY-THREE – How does one explain the actions of a horrendous act? Why is there so much sin, evil, bitterness, hurt and heartache? Some questions may never be answered in this life. Why do people do such horrible things to each other? Our need to know can actually destroy us mentally and spiritually. Why God allows or doesn't allow something to happen? I do not know. What I know for sure, God has a plan. He is watching, He is preparing, He is supreme, He will have justice, and He will win. He is Sovereign, Holy, and all knowing. He just wants us to trust Him – we are not God. Just trust and obey, for there really is no other way to live a stress free, tension free, anxiety free life.

The Tithe

Ron was an airmen first class and I was pregnant with our first child. We were scheduled to move on base in six months, but that didn't help us with our immediate problem – no money! We were faced with a decision. If we tithed (ten percent of our income) we could pay our bills, but no money for food. It was going to be a long two weeks. We lived pay check to pay check and we were seriously down to saltine crackers and peanut butter.

My first thought, "Let's call our parents", but Ron said, "No". We would not call either of our parents, again. Ron said we needed to trust God and He would provide. I agreed, but still, I was hungry just thinking about those stale crackers and scraping the jar of peanut butter. The decision was made, we would not tell anyone, and continue to pray, and trust God. That was Saturday, on Sunday we tithed, and on Monday it happened.

Throughout the day, starting early in the morning, families started dropping off bags of groceries. I remember feeling embarrassed and saying we were fine, but the first older lady ignored me completely until she put the last bag of groceries on the kitchen table. She said she took her "orders" from God and He impressed on her heart during the morning service. She said, "He told us to bring you groceries".

She said this may be humbling now, but one day I'll be able to help someone and then I will have the sensitivity to share with them a blessing of God's mercy and grace. We had families bringing bags of glorious food all day long. Each family shared the same story, during Sunday morning service, after the offering.

God spoke to their hearts about bringing groceries to our house. When Ron came home, I asked him if he had told anybody about our financial situation. But Ron or I had not shared our lack of funds with anybody. Ron had some good news too. There was an early opening for housing on base. We could move in immediately. We ended up having enough food for almost two months. I have never forgotten that lesson on being humble and passing it forward.

SCRIPTURE:

"But this I say; he who sows sparingly, will also reap sparingly, and he who sows bountifully will also reap bountifully. So let each one give as he purposes in his heart, not grudgingly or of necessity; for God loves a cheerful giver." II Corinthians 9: 6-7 (NKJV)

WORDS OF ENCOURAGEMENT FOR THE WEEK:

DAY TWO HUNDRED NINETY-FOUR – Life is full of "I wish I had" – It's not too late; make it a day to say, "I'm glad I did."

DAY TWO HUNDRED NINETY-FIVE – God knows you want it, but are you ready to receive it?

DAY TWO HUNDRED NINETY-SIX – The Gift
The gift was free from Him you see,
the cost was very high,
they took His life on Calvary
to save a wretched soul like me.
My heart I gave to Him that day,
never more to roam,
very soon I too will stand,
before the great White Throne.
In my defense one will arise

and take His place along my side,
"her sins were washed away this day,
for she did repent along the way".
The King of kings will look around;
on that very day,
"Welcome home He'll say at last,
"for you are glory bound".
For you accepted my Son that day,
and now the trumpet sounds.
"Well done thy good and faithful child"
come here to me, and accept your crown.

DAY TWO HUNDRED NINETY-SEVEN – Since the beginning of time you were meant to be. As God was creating the heavens and the earth, you were on His mind. He has always known your weaknesses, your strengths, and potential. His hope, His joy, and the love of His life - has always been YOU!

DAY TWO HUNDRED NINETY-EIGHT – Pam and Kevin invited us to a BBQ on that festive 4th of July weekend back in '94. I had selected the cutest red, white and blue outfit. We were outside enjoying the day of fellowship with our dear friends, when all of sudden, a bird flies by and poops right on me. I must have a bull's eye on me that read "The poop stops here". I have to say, I was irritated. My brand new outfit would never be the same. I went inside to wash up and then came back out and moved our chairs. My friends were very kind, at least to my face, about the entire incident. Within five minutes of sitting back down I got bombed again…I was in disbelief. My friends, who had been so kind the first time, could no longer control their laughter, and didn't even try to hide the laugh out loud moment. I have to admit, the odds were in my favor, and I was on a roll. Before long, everyone was laughing at this unexpected turn of events. It's been twenty years and we still laugh about it. I had a choice, I could have stayed mad, gone home, or just pouted for the rest of the day. But laughter was by far the best choice for me to make. What can you laugh about today?

DAY TWO HUNDRED NINETY-NINE – You are not a mistake. You, my friend, are a walking - talking miracle.

DAY THREE HUNDRED – We have felt the pain, but we can push against it and rise again. We have cried the tears, letting us release the ache in our hearts. We mourn them still, and we always will, but we will honor their memory today. The cut is so deep, but in time we will wear the scars of our heart and know we are survivors. Bringing comfort and understanding to others. I will choose today to get up, cry if I want to, honor their memory, and look around to see who needs a kind word, a cup of tea, or a hand of comfort. God leaves us behind because our work here is not yet done. We have a destiny to fulfill. He holds our loved ones in His arms until our work here is finally done. In memory of those dear to my heart that have gone home to be with the Lord.

Unholy prayers

I had been offended, he yelled at me and I cried all morning. It was the late summer of '76 and our landlord had to speak to us once again about our dog. Who doesn't like dogs? Our landlord seemed so hateful, and I HATED him, that old man was just plain mean and hurtful. God, are you watching? He is hurting one of your children, ME!

I spent the afternoon looking up scripture. If only I had that kind of zeal to find scripture on God's grace and mercy. I finally found a scripture that I liked and could quote all day long. I was hoping God would hear me.

Luke 17:2 (NKJV) – "It would be better for him if a millstone were hung around his neck, and he were thrown into the sea, than that he should offend one of these little ones." I quoted that scripture, I cried that God would make him shut up, and I never wanted to hear his voice AGAIN. I hated him, I wanted him to die (have you ever had those thoughts?). No? Well, I was young, immature, and had no clue to the real power of PRAYER. So, I thought naturally God should hate him too. *The mind of a very immature Christian and I am still ashamed that I prayed this prayer.

The following morning the phone rang, it was our landlord's wife. She was obviously very upset. Last night, around 11:00 p.m. Edmond, her husband, had collapsed. She called the doctor and he said Edmond had had a stroke last night, it was quite serious. Even if he does recover he will most likely never speak again. She knew we were Christians and she was hoping that we would put her husband on the prayer chain at our church. I still feel the great shame of that moment in my Christian faith. Because someone hurt my feelings, I wanted them dead or in some type of pain. I almost fell to the floor, I was immediately convicted, shamed, and worse than that; God was watching me. Oh Lord, forgive me, forgive him, I prayed. I called the church office to put him on the prayer chain. He did recover after many months, but he walked with a cane and never spoke again to my knowledge.

I can't stress this portion enough, praying is not random, it is not to get God to strike someone down that we don't like and it is not as a last resort. Prayer is sacred. Prayer is a holy time between you and God almighty. Prayer is life changing and can result in life changing matters. Prayer is to edify, to bring glory to God, to sustain us, to comfort us, to restore us, and to humble us. Prayer is for healing us and others but above all, our prayers are to have an intimate relationship with our heavenly Father.

*I prayed this as a baby Christian, not knowing the ramifications of what prayer really was, but to pray this now I believe God would deal with me harshly and now that you know too, the same goes for you.

SCRIPTURE:

> "But I say to you, love your enemies, bless those who curse you, do good to those who hate you, and pray for those who spitefully use you and persecute you, that you may be sons of your Father in heaven; for He makes His sunrise on the evil and on the good and sends rain on the just and on the unjust. For if you love those who love you, what reward have you? Do not even the tax collectors do the same? Matthew 5: 44-46 (NKJV)

WORDS OF ENCOURAGEMENT FOR THE WEEK:

DAY THREE HUNDRED ONE – Holy Week
Blessed is the Holy week
blessed are the very meek.
Blessed is my family dears
blessed are the ones so near.
Blessed is the cheerful heart

blessed are His works of art.
Blessed are my dearest friends
blessed are the great weekends.
Blessed is the new day dawning
blessed are the ones He's calling.

DAY THREE HUNDRED TWO – At your lowest point the devil will do his best to convince you that you are a failure. He will say you are unlovable, and that God hasn't heard you. Time to turn the tide – at your lowest point remember you are on a threshold of greatness. You will inspire everyone around you, and God not only has heard you, but He whispers in your ear "I love you". Keep the faith beloved, you never walk alone – Think it, speak it, and share it!

DAY THREE HUNDRED THREE – This week could have been the worst week ever for you. This week could have been filled with anxiety and stress. This week could have felt like God was not even hearing your prayers. On the other hand, this week could have been the best week ever for you. This week could have given you peace and joy. This week could have felt like God answered all your prayers in record time. Next week your roles could be reversed – what's the difference? There is no difference. God is still with you whether you are having a horrible week or a fantastic week. He is here, holding your hand and cheering you on. Praise Him no matter what kind of week you're having. Don't let the week determine how you feel, for it can change in an instant. A sign that you are growing up spiritually is that you don't let your situation dictate how you are feeling.

DAY THREE HUNDRED FOUR – I will choose to breakthrough with the power of God in my life. I will not base what I am capable of doing by looking in the mirror – for my physical being is only the shell. I will tap in to the light of my soul, for the darkness cannot penetrate through. By exposing the light into the open, I have broken the ties of bondage and I am now free to be seen as God sees me.

DAY THREE HUNDRED FIVE – I find myself awake again in the middle of the night. Is this the only time God can get my attention? Can I only truly hear His voice when the silence is the loudest? Is a full night of uninterrupted sleep a thing of the past? Is this the new norm? My mind quiets and a thought crosses my mind, "stop over thinking it." "Everything has a season". "Growth comes at a price". "Be still and know that I AM."

DAY THREE HUNDRED SIX – Every day since the beginning, during our nap time, I would hold my little one in my arms and quietly pray over her. One day when I got up to get lunch ready, she crawled in my spot on the couch. When I came back, I teased her by asking if she was the Nana now. She started to giggle and said, "yes, I Nana." So, I sat in her spot and told her I was her peanut. She thought that was so funny. Then she carefully took my head and placed it on her left shoulder. She placed her right hand on my head and quietly mumbled to God. I could not understand what she was saying, but I know God heard her prayers and understood every word.

DAY THREE HUNDRED SEVEN – I believe in the Father, the Son, and the Holy Spirit. I believe the Bible is the Holy Word of God and I believe Jesus died on the cross for the world and for me. He is global and personal. I believe prayer is our greatest weapon. I simply believe!

CHAPTER ELEVEN

MY WALK IN FAITH

My Destiny

"I can't marry you" my future husband said to me on the phone. In the two years we were engaged, the only thing we would argue about was religion. He had "found" God in Mountain Home, Idaho and I thought I was doing okay on my own. Well, I wasn't going to let a little thing like religion stop me from getting married. Next week I told Ron I had seen the light, and the wedding was back on. Fast forward to the wedding night, and sleeping together for the first time. I was abruptly woken up to Ron screaming and kicking me. I had often wondered what the people in the next room thought of the man screaming in fear. Ron jumped out of bed, obviously shaken up. He told me he had watched me go into the bathroom then suddenly something evil grabbed him from behind and whispered in his ear, "I will destroy your family". I remember thinking, "okay, so far married life is not that fun, and mom sure didn't tell me about this part of marriage". I guess I was wearing my "what the heck are you talking about?" face. Ron took my hand and said, "I am so grateful we are both saved". Without looking at him I said, "Oh yeah, me too". We did end up sleeping with the light on for the rest of the night, after all, I was only eighteen and Ron was nineteen years old. Side note: We actually had to show our marriage certificate to the hotel manager before they gave us a room key.

The next morning at breakfast Ron had some great news. For one night only, only one hour away, there was an old time tent revival meeting and he knew I would love to go. Oh, holy smoke, was he kidding me? Who goes to church on their honeymoon? I tried my best to get out of it, but in the end we went. He promised me a Maine lobster dinner first, for after all I had to get something out of it.

So in we go, sitting on the bleachers in the back. Never in my life had I ever experienced such a thing. The preacher was dressed in black pants with black suspenders, black tie, stark white shirt, sleeves rolled up to his elbows, and he held the biggest Bible in one hand and a white handkerchief in the other. I was hypnotized, watching him walk back and forth, as he held the Bible in the air and wiping the sweat off his brow with the other. He turned, pointed right at me, and said "REPENT"! Everyone, bow your heads and close your eyes, as he gave the plan of salvation. He asked for the commitment to follow Christ, raise your hand. I did, and before I knew it someone was by my side, getting me to go with them.

I thought they were kicking me out, the heathen that I was. Ron just stared at me and waved goodbye. I guess I deserved this, since I lied to Ron. I was getting what I deserved, the boot. I went in a room of about fifteen young people and about ten altar workers, who were born again Christians. We bowed our heads and prayed the sinner's prayer. When I lifted my head I looked around, I knew something was different, even though I didn't totally understand it. For the first time I understood there was a difference between religion and needing Jesus, not because I did anything wonderful or deserving, but simply because He loved me and I accepted the gift, the gift of salvation.

Even though I had been brought up in church, I never understood that I needed to make it personal. I was just going through the motions, until that night, when I realized Jesus could be my Lord and Savior. Please let me stress this point before I accepted Jesus in my heart I was raised in a Christian and loving home. My problem was that I didn't want to go beyond that. My religion, or my parents, couldn't save me. Only accepting Jesus into my heart and making Him my Lord and Savior could do that. I had to make it personal and I will be forever grateful I did.

SCRIPTURE:

> "that if you confess with your mouth the Lord Jesus and believe in your heart that God has raised Him from the dead, you will be saved. For with the heart one believes unto righteousness, and with the mouth confession is made unto salvation." Romans 10: 9-10 (NKJV)

WORDS OF ENCOURAGEMENT FOR THE WEEK:

DAY THREE HUNDRED EIGHT – The beautiful face doesn't prove someone is good or kind. The material wealth doesn't mean they are financially secure, or seeing someone in church every week doesn't mean they are going to heaven. Look past the physical being and see what God sees. Trust the spiritual senses God has given you.

DAY THREE HUNDRED NINE – My time was now, I could feel the change transforming me. My very core would soon be tested. Yes, it all makes sense now, the unexplained illnesses, the unexpected financial bills, betrayal of friendships, and the whispers of evil. Not seeing with my eyes, nevertheless my physical senses were telling me to stay alert. I could so easily give in to the fear, the gut wrenching pit in my stomach. Yet, through the darkness, the voice of peace is ever louder. "Be still and know that I AM." The spiritual warfare had begun and I was about to see a glimpse of evil, the spirit of grace, and what I truly look like behind the curtain.

This is the start of my novel, how does yours begin? We all have a novel inside us. Take the time to see how yours is being written today.

DAY THREE HUNDRED TEN – Have you done everything humanly possible? If you have worked as hard as you could work, if you have said all there was to say – Now stop! God is in control, He has a plan. Look to Him and pray. Pray for our leaders for every seat in our government, God has a plan. We just need to keep our eyes on Him. Stop your complaining, the only thing you will accomplish is to turn the lost away from the light!

DAY THREE HUNDRED ELEVEN – If all ways are possible to heaven, then why did Jesus have to die on the cross?

DAY THREE HUNDRED TWELVE – Are you too old to begin a new journey? Have you passed your prime to start a new project? Are you too set in your ways to come out of your comfort zone? No, you are now aged to perfection and you have the right ingredients to stay balanced. You are on the same journey as before, but now God has opened the gates to a new path. Now your spiritual gifts will burst forth in ways you can't even imagine. God has not forgotten you, your time has now come. Your comfort will come when He brings you home. Now is the perfect time, one moment sooner, and you would have not been ready.

DAY THREE HUNDRED THIRTEEN – Have you ever experienced a holy time in your life? While standing on the fourteenth floor of a very large ship, I had the honor of watching the sunrise. As the sun began to slowly rise up over the horizon and the vastness of the ocean, I found myself praising His name. Overwhelmed with how majestic this scene was. When I closed my eyes I swear I could hear the orchestra of heaven playing in the rhythm of the rising sun. It's that simple and that complicated all in a wonderful moment.

DAY THREE HUNDRED FOURTEEN – Praise and Prayer have all the power. Believe in who you are talking to.

Crossing the line

No one escapes this life without hurt and suffering. We live in an imperfect world with imperfect human beings. We all make mistakes, we all fall down, and we all need Christ to give us a hand up and going again. Sometimes we love someone so much and we want to help them so desperately during a difficult time that we cross the line into God's territory. This is not good for them or for you.

How do you know when you've crossed the line? Are you racked with guilt over it? Does your mind play the problem over and over again? Is their problem now your problem? Is it all you think about? Are you shouldering the blame for someone else? Have you become physically ill over their problem? No wonder you are ill, because you are trying to do God's job. It's not YOUR cross to bear. You need to step back from their problem, take a deep breath, and let it go. Do you want to help them? Pray for them. You don't think that's enough? You are wrong! Prayer holds the secrets to the universe. Prayer will change the heart of the lost. Prayer is your greatest weapon against evil in this world. Evil's job is to take down your loved ones, and if evil can, it will take you down too.

You are not helping your loved ones by trying to carry someone else's load, if anything you're going to multiply the problem and quite possibly block God's flow. When I asked a dear Christian friend how I could help my loved ones, she told me that I needed to leave the problem with God, and then "mind my own business". It's between God and them. Great words of wisdom for my well being and I am so grateful I had those words spoken to me.

I gave it to God and received peace of mind, joy of heart, and quiet to my soul. Your only job is to pray. Pray in your car, at the altar, in the spirit, in your closet, fasting, on your knees, pray even if you can't see any results – PRAY!

SCRIPTURE:

"Peace I leave with you; my peace I give you. I do not give to you as the world gives. Do not let your hearts be troubled and do not be afraid." John 14:27 (NIV)

WORDS OF ENCOURAGEMENT FOR THE WEEK:

DAY THREE HUNDRED FIFTEEN – I rise this morning knowing I have been given another opportunity – I have been entrusted to complete what I was meant to do – I will not dwell on the what ifs, the why nots, or the how comes. It is none of my business – mankind is my business and I will focus there today.

DAY THREE HUNDRED SIXTEEN – Even if no one acknowledges you doing a great job at work – HE WILL. Even if no one sees you caring for your elderly parents – HE SEES. Even if no one thanks you for caring for an ill friend – HE DOES. Even if no one understands how hard it is – HE KNOWS!

DAY THREE HUNDRED SEVENTEEN – Any good seen in me comes from Him. Any kindness acted out from me is from Him. Any good word written or spoken from me comes from Him. Any inspiration, hope or love from me started first with Him. Any complaining comes from me. Any prideful act comes straight from me. Any impatience comes directly through me. Any ignorance, hatred or jealously sparks out of me. I am a work in progress, certainly not perfect by any means, but I will continue to get up, seek His face and try, try again. Lord, take out the me today and replace it with You.

DAY THREE HUNDRED EIGHTEEN – The NO's of this world will not deter me from what I have been called to do. My heart is willing, my mind is preparing, and my body...well, two out of three ain't bad. All kidding aside, don't be discouraged by the negative Nellie's of this world! YOU COUNT!

DAY THREE HUNDRED NINETEEN – What are you re-enforcing today? Are you going down the same road that has led you nowhere? Will you break the mold of destruction and see yourself as the person you were meant to become? This is no ordinary day, not for you. Today, the blinders will come off. You will hear what needs to be said, and you will begin a new season in your life! My prayer for you is that you will see what I see in you – a miracle!

DAY THREE HUNDRED TWENTY – Jesus is the same Savior for all. What makes this so simple and so complicated? Everyone's testimony/experience's are different and uniquely their own. All different stories – all same results.

DAY THREE HUNDRED TWENTY-ONE – In the face of turmoil I can now see calmness. In the face of sadness I can experience joy. In the face of crying I am able to remember the laughter. In the face of rejection I now stand on His strength. In the face of anger I am filled with His peace, and in the face of loneliness I look for compassion. My hope for you today is that you will choose the path that will enrich your life, and more importantly, the lives around you.

Giving up

I had stopped going to church, I let the anger build up, and I became what I said. I was now a bitter, disappointed, and hurt Christian. When the problems came more and more frequently, the more I pulled back and gave up. I stopped listening to God's voice and started listening to the devil's whispers.

The walls of self-pity, hurt, and bitterness had now been formed, growing each day until after ten years it was a massive building indeed. When we moved the final time, I had such a difficult time finding just the right church. Our last church was small and I left dear friends, what church could compare? I started to miss services and I was surprised how easy it was to miss more and more Sundays. After all, I worked and I needed my rest. Even if I didn't go, it's not like anyone would miss me, except my husband, who continued on going. My Bible reading was non-existent and my prayer time was but a few sentences long.

My joy was gone and for the next ten years I lived with a pit in my stomach. I was actually getting quite comfortable in my invisible prison. The pit in my gut was now a way of life. I carried a chip on my shoulder that I wore with pride. I was useless in sharing the good news of Christ. My testimony was gone and I didn't care, BUT HE did. Through a series of events that seemed harder and harder to recover from, I finally reached out to a new Christian, who was my old boss, my friend, Roxene. Even though I said I didn't care, my spirit was crying out for fellowship and I desperately missed my relationship with my heavenly Father. I told Roxene I had no interest in large churches since I found them impersonal and hypocritical. So, she simply invited me to come to a life group, a small intimate group where you can share some Bible lessons. There was no joining a church, no commitment, and no one to judge me.

I decided I would go. I was so spiritually dry and my soul was desperate to hear the word of God. I was at a spiritual crossroad. Have you ever been in a spiritual crossroad? Have you ever been hurt by church or by comments of a self righteous Christian?

Maybe you just can't believe that so many awful things have happened to you in your life and you think God has let you down. Is that the case? Whatever the reason may be, know that God does have a plan for your life, He loves you right where you are and He believes in you.

"Return, you backsliding children, And I will heal your backslidings." Jeremiah 3:22 (NKJV)

WORDS OF ENCOURAGEMENT FOR THE WEEK:

DAY THREE HUNDRED TWENTY-TWO – Until you change your mind set, nothing will change in your life.

DAY THREE HUNDRED TWENTY-THREE – You can't force someone to turn to God. God will speak to the individual heart when the heart is ready to hear His voice. Only God knows the exact timing. You need to leave it at the altar and let God do what He does best – save the soul, all in His timing. What is your job? Keep praying, keep believing, and keep praising. He answered your prayer the moment you spoke it.

DAY THREE HUNDRED TWENTY-FOUR – The memories are bittersweet, for at first they haunt us. Each one that passes through our mind reminding us of what is now gone and the ache in our heart threatens to destroy our very core. But as the time passes by, and others get on with the business of living, when their name isn't part of the conversation anymore, we can take solace in the memories. We will never forget the touch, the laugh, the smile, and the pure joy of their life. We can hold on to these precious memories until once again we are united with our loved ones on the other side of grace.

DAY THREE HUNDRED TWENTY-FIVE – When my daughter, Jessy, was in the sixth grade, someone told her she was poor because she got free lunches at school. She shot right back saying,"

No, free lunches are one of our military benefits because my Dad is serving in the military". There are some things worth trading off for. Serving our Country and not having much material wise gave my kids the gumption for their values and have brought them through many a difficult time. My children developed an appreciation for even the smallest rewards. Don't be upset or sad because you can't give your loved ones their hearts desire. This could end up being their greatest gift in life.

DAY THREE HUNDRED TWENTY-SIX – Lord change the heart of my enemies, forgive them; but also protect us from those who plan evil against us. Let there be a hedge of protection around my family. Shelter us from the storms that threaten to destroy us. Continue to change my heart that I would see the good in my enemies and love them where they are.

DAY THREE HUNDRED TWENTY-SEVEN – As the year ends once more – before I can make any commitments for the New Year, I must first clean out my spiritual house. Putting out the negative, the unresolved feelings, the pride of thinking I must do it alone, and the fear of trying something new. I will understand change is necessary to get to the next level. I am stronger than I thought, setting my mind for courage, and preparing for the blessings. I will not continually look back, but forge ahead with a renewed spirit. I have a journey to complete, let's break through, for our time has come.

DAY THREE HUNDRED TWENTY-EIGHT – It's time to grow up my brothers and sisters. Answer in Love – Respond in Kindness – React with a smile – When in doubt be silent – Act in joy

– Behave in a way that you know God is watching – Ignore the physical; and seek the heart – Forgiveness is the root needed to bring you into spiritual adulthood.

Redemption

Have you ever hit a spiritual rock bottom? Have you forgotten how to listen for His voice? Have you ever sat in your car and asked God to give you a sign? Have you ever rung the door bell on the first night of your first life group and felt totally alone? I was meeting people for the first time when the hostess put her arms around me and whispered in my ear, "welcome home". I have said this many times while sharing my testimony, "Life Group saved my spiritual life". Life Group was the stepping stone in turning my spiritual life around. Side note: The hostess doesn't remember saying that to me, but I remember it was such an odd statement for someone to say the first time to their house. I personally believe it was the Holy Spirit whispering in my ear.

My guard was up, and I wasn't going to be hurt again. But in spite of me, the Lord led me to the perfect group. So humble, so compassionate, and non judgmental, the perfect place to be fed the word of God. Our leaders loved us right where we were, which was rock bottom for me. They cared more about how we were doing than what we were doing. How refreshing to be ministered to in this way. Everyone in our group came with a story, a heartache, and a testimony to share. The most humble group I have ever had the pleasure of knowing.

For the next four months the self imposed prison walls were coming down around me and I felt stronger. Was I finally ready to attend church? It would be different for me. I wasn't use to their kind of music, the raising of hands, and praising out loud. Could I handle that? Our friends were waiting for us in the lobby. They saved us a seat, okay, so far, so good. There was a meet and greet immediately after the service and I could feel the walls trying to go back up. First person I met was Joy. She introduced herself and asked me if I was new to the area. I shot right back, "No, I've backslid for the past ten years." Joy never missed a beat, she gently touched my arm, and while smiling she said, "I am so glad you are here this morning." I studied her face to see it there was even a hint of judgment, and there was none.

We joined the church in 2005 and I can honestly say I am home now. You can even see me during the praise and worship raising my arms up in jubilee and saying a hearty amen. What I had forgotten was that church was my inspiration point to start my week. Church offered me a place to worship, a place for prayer, learning God's Word, and support in all matters. We have been blessed along the way with our own Life Group and we have watched it grow and multiply. God is so good and faithful!

SCRIPTURE:

"The son said to him, Father, I have sinned against heaven and against you. I am no longer worthy to be called your son. But the Father said to his servants, Quick, bring the best robe and put it on him. Put a ring on his finger, and sandals on his feet. Bring the fattened calf and kill it. Let's have a feast and celebrate. For this son of mine was dead and is alive again; he was lost and is found. So they began to celebrate." Luke 15: 21-24 (NIV)

WORDS OF ENCOURAGEMENT FOR THE WEEK:

DAY THREE HUNDRED TWENTY-NINE – The day is set before me. How will I choose to live it? Will I be joyful or complain? Will I be grateful or find fault? Will I be kind or hurtful? Will I hold my tongue or gossip? Will I smile or grumble? I have been given a gift. Will I accept it or throw it away? In my words, let me choose them wisely, in my thoughts, let me think lovingly, in my actions, let them see I care. At the end of the day, let God be my Master.

DAY THREE HUNDRED THIRTY – Quit fighting against the storm, you are there for a reason. Learn what the storm is trying to teach you, for soon the winds will push you in the direction you were meant to shine. You will be the beacon in the dark, you will lift the hopeless out of the valley, and you will share the good news of Christ. God's ways are not our ways. He wants us to learn all we can so we can move up the spiritual ladder of holiness.

DAY THREE HUNDRED THIRTY-ONE – Why the hurt, the pain, and the heartbreak? Out of the trials of this life are born perseverance, endurance, and compassion into our very being. In the trenches of a trial you will learn to reach out and begin anew. You will begin to understand the servant's heart, and humbly approach the day. Without the negative of this life there would be no balance to your spirit. Soon you will begin to see that the experience of a troubled season will reap a harvest of a glorious new beginning.

DAY THREE HUNDRED THIRTY-TWO – When you go to the altar to confess your sin(s), remember God takes those sins and throws them away. If you're still racked with guilt, it is of the devil, not God. It's time to kick that old devil to the curb.

DAY THREE HUNDRED THIRTY-THREE – When Ron and I were dating and he was stationed miles away in the military, we would write each other every day. My mother told me to never write anything that I wouldn't want her to read. I could always visualize her standing behind me, a great visual for all kids/adults to use. I would like to add caution in the new millennium when sending pictures and texting. Remember mother is watching – and more importantly, God is watching!

DAY THREE HUNDRED THIRTY-FOUR – Your eyes tell the story of your hidden courage and strength. You don't have to settle. You are a treasure to behold. Your smile lights up the entire room. You are a blessing to all who meet you. If you don't believe me, ask God.

DAY THREE HUNDRED THIRTY-FIVE – It was parent/teacher conferences at the children's school in 1987. At the dinner table, the night before the conferences, I announced to my children that if they had something they needed to tell me now would be the time. My son, Josh, was in the second grade and he started to look very worried. As I continued talking, I could see Josh was now squirming in his seat. He was not at all comfortable with this conversation. I prepared myself to hear his confession. "Josh, if something has happened at school, you must tell me now", I said. "You know mommy doesn't like surprises, so start talking." The entire table got quiet. Jess and Jason seemed a little too happy to hear what kind of trouble their little brother might be getting into. Josh's eyes were cast down, sweat was forming over his top lip. "Mommy," he said, "I have to tell you something." I braced myself. "Mommy, my teacher has a mustache and please, please, PLEASE don't tell her I told you!" At the conference I did as Josh had requested. I did not mention her mustache, although any man would have been proud to sport such a magnificent display of hair between the nose and lip.

CHAPTER TWELVE

IN THE AUTUMN OF MY LIFE

Looking in the Mirror

Standing in front of my mirror I no longer see the young girl I once was. I barely recognize this person standing in front of me. Instead of a girl, I now see the reflection of a woman. Upon inspection I see wrinkles around her eyes, letting me know that she laughed more than she cried. Her arms have gotten full and soft, yet they are strong and she is still able to cradle her grand-children to her chest.

Alas, something I finally see that belongs to me, those dreaded stretch marks which I use to despise, but now I see them and smile. They bring with them the memories of carrying my babies inside me and giving birth to my four children. The gray seems to multiply throughout my hair faster than I care to admit, but it lets me know that I have weathered the storms of life and I'm still here.

SCRIPTURE:

"I will give thanks to you for I am fearfully and wonder-fully made; wonderful are your works and my soul knows it very well." Psalm 139:14 (NASB)

DAY THREE HUNDRED THIRTY-SIX – Did you know that God keeps our prayers in a golden bowl? "And when he had taken it, the four living creatures and the twenty-four elders fell down before the Lamb, Jesus. Each one had a harp and they were holding golden bowls full of incense, which are the prayers of the saints." Revelation 5:8 (NIV) Tell me again why you think our prayers don't matter – you see my friend, your prayers mean everything to God. Let us praise His holy name and pray.

DAY THREE HUNDRED THIRTY-SEVEN – Just because I don't understand the answer, the judgment, or the silence, I don't have to know to trust Him. I don't have to know to experience joy, and I don't have to know the plan. I can only speak from my own personal experience, but He has given me peace in my heart. He speaks to my soul, and I sense His love and plan for my life. As I trusted my parents to care for me when I was young, I never asked them how they were going to take care of me. I just accepted it and knew they did. Turn your heart and mind over to God, He never disappoints.

DAY THREE HUNDRED THIRTY-EIGHT – I believe God has laid on my heart to begin a ministry here in South Carolina, called CLAP YOUR HANDS. We make therapy puppets/socks, tabs, bibs and weighted blankets/vests for kids who have physical limitations in their life. I always find it amusing how God will use ideas and ministries, and use people who have no idea what they are doing, and make something glorious out of it. I believe, God, laid on my heart to buy a sewing machine and learn to sew. He surrounded me with gifted and giving seamstresses and professionals who have guided us through the process of making the best possible items for "our" kids. I have in my chapter, teenagers and ladies, even in their eighties, all working together to make a difference in a child's life. I am once again reminded, nothing is impossible with God. What is God calling you to do? Remember, even if you have no experience, God will put the knowledge into your mind, and bring you angels to accomplish His will. These are exciting times my friend!

DAY THREE HUNDRED THIRTY-NINE – Ushering in the presence of God always begins with praise, singing, and worship. Throughout time, throughout the Bible, this is the starting point of favor with the Holy Spirit.

DAY THREE HUNDRED FORTY – As spring approaches, my thoughts turn to starting my spiritual garden. My heavenly Father has already prepared the soil and the patch of ground He wants me to work over. He has given me the tools of spiritual gifts and the seeds of kindness, love, hope, and encouragement. All I have to do is plant the seeds and make sure I water them. As the gardener, I must watch out for those gossips, complainers, and vengeful spirits who threaten to eat all I have planted. If this happens to you, I suggest the old faithful remedies of placing prayer and praise all around the perimeters of your garden. Before you know it, your garden will be flourishing and it will be time to harvest what you have planted. If you have any questions, please feel free to ask the Head gardener, God. Have a great planting season my friends!

DAY THREE HUNDRED FORTY-ONE – It's a simple prayer – the prayer of salvation. I prayed – Lord, I am sinner, I am asking you to forgive my sins. I understand Your Son, Jesus, died on the cross for my sins and only through Him can I be forgiven. John

14:6 (NIV) "Jesus answered, "I am the way and the truth and the life. No one comes to the Father except through me."

Lord, wash my sins away with the blood of Jesus. Come into my heart Jesus to live forever. Dear Father, thank you for saving me.

Romans10:13 (NKJV) " For whoever calls on the name of the Lord will be saved."

Not because I deserve it at all, it's all because of the shedding of blood on the cross. I thank you Lord for Your mercy, grace, and redemption power.

DAY THREE HUNDRED FORTY-TWO – The world will throw you a bone, but God will make you feast. The world wants to put you up in a cheap motel, but God wants you to stay in a castle. The world only asks you questions, but God will supply you with the answers. The world will use you up, but God will fill you up. The world will disappoint you, but God never will.

You are stronger than you think

I can't remember the last time I had physically worked so hard to get a home improvement job done. We began prepping the walls, ripping down wallpaper, scrubbing the baseboards, and taping the corners around the bathroom and master bedroom. Next we began the process of priming the first walls, then going up and down the ladder several times, and finally putting on the first coat of paint. We ended up skipping supper and finally crashing on the couch around 9:00 p.m. Every muscle in my body hurt, where was the Ben-Gay? I managed to finally sit down with a glass of milk and a Hershey candy bar.

As I sat there on the couch, I seriously debated just sleeping where I was, but I knew I would just be adding to the pain of a cramped neck. As I headed upstairs, each step I climbed hurt. I was walking like I was ninety, but I didn't care, the pain, the pain. Looking at the bed and then at myself, I debated, whether or not to change out of my clothes. Oh why couldn't I just be spontane-ous and just fall into bed? As I slowly headed to the bathroom to change, out of the corner of my eye I saw the biggest palmetto bug on my shirt. These are the most disgusting bugs, they are big, gross, and they fly. What could I do? I had to go into survival mode. I started to scream, I clawed, and I jumped high into the air. I pulled and twisted, moving in such way as to impress any gymnast.

As I was slapping myself, trying to rip the shirt off my back, I happen to look in the mirror. Hmm, I noticed that it was not a palmetto bug after all, but a piece of Hershey candy that must have fallen on my shirt. Out of breath and thankful for the candy and not the bug, I looked into the mirror and realized I guess I wasn't as tired as I thought I was. Lesson learned: Even though you feel like you are on your last bit of strength, there is always a reserve – push through, I believe in you.

SCRIPTURE:

"He gives strength to the weary, and increases the power of the weak." Isaiah 40:29 (NIV)

DAY THREE HUNDRED FORTY-THREE – When we are sick, physically, we know that we need to rest, take plenty of fluids and listen to our doctor to get well. If we don't take care of our bodies, they will fall apart and complicate an otherwise regular illness. When we are sick spiritually, we don't always see the signs so clearly. Some ways we can spot a potential spiritual illness is to see if we are stressed out, worried sick, and anxiety filling our hearts. These are just the symptoms of a more serious issue. God is the great healer of our souls. He will bring peace to your mind and joy to your heart. He even makes house calls. Trust Him to help you, to heal you, and to restore you to the person you were meant to be.

DAY THREE HUNDRED FORTY-FOUR – Our prayers have always been for complete healing, complete redemption, complete financial freedom, and complete protection from our enemies. Prepare yourself, God's path for our life may take some twists and turns and we need to allow God to use all things, and in all situations, to bring glory to Him. It's not about us. It's about helping others, serving, and showing compassion on a world that has forgotten how to respond to the hopeless, the fallen, and the lost.

DAY THREE HUNDRED FORTY-FIVE – About ten years ago, Ron and I were trying to work out and have a healthier life style. However, we were near Ron's work and Burger King was so convenient to just grab something quick. Ron reluctantly agreed and I felt like the weak link until we got inside. As we approached the front counter, there to greet us was an older woman, all smiles and saying "hi" to Ron. I said, "How does she know you?" He shrugged and said, "He may occasionally come in for breakfast". He barely got out the sentence when the cashier yelled out to her fellow workers that "Ron was in the house". Everyone came out from behind the back room to say "hey" to Ron. "So you barely come here?" He sheepishly looked down and said, "He may come in every morning for a quick bite". I had to once again remember that if you do something in private it will come to light eventually.

DAY THREE HUNDRED FORTY-SIX – The problems in this life will change and mold us into the person we are meant to become. Sometimes, if we're not careful, we can let our problems take on a life of their own. How you see your problem can be a problem. It's but a stepping stone to a higher calling. Don't let the problem rule over you, but simply use the problem to walk closer to God. Add these to form the fabric of your testimony. You can own the problem and not the other way around.

DAY THREE HUNDRED FORTY-SEVEN – What is a season? A season can be beautiful, full of wonder and rebirth. A season can be full of travel, and a time to explore the world. A season can be a time to reflect, a time of harvest and a time to reap the blessings. A season can be cold, dark, and on some days unable to see what lies ahead. Seasons all have the same number of days but sometimes, if we're not careful, we can become stuck in a season. This is not how the world works. We must go through each season so we can get to the next one. A season has a certain amount of days in it. It will soon pass and you will enter into the next season of your life. Stop looking at the season you are in as the final destination – it's not! I would like to add that the season that is cold, dark, and difficult to see ahead – this is also the season where heroes are born! Every season can be used for His glory.

DAY THREE HUNDRED FORTY-EIGHT – I will not complain because it insults God. I will not complain because it does no good. I will not complain because it weakens my faith. I will not complain because I woke up this morning. I will not complain because I chose to count my blessings. I will not complain because it throws a negative energy all around me. I will not complain because today could be the day it all turns around.

DAY THREE HUNDRED FORTY-NINE – A good word - A word of praise - A prayer. A good Word (I believe the Word is scripture) opens the gate to God's Kingdom. A moment of praise sends the angels to our side. A prayer on our lips explodes the Heavenly realms to endless possibilities.

The day before the movers came

Even though we had professional movers coming to pack us up and move us across the Country, we still had a lot of prep time. We had to figure out what to send with the movers, what to throw away, and what to physically take with us. We still had so much to do, especially with four small children who desperately wanted to help us. Ron and I kept switching off kids. We would just start getting into something, when the kids would begin whining about something we were trying to throw away, or they were hungry or they would start fighting with each other. These were the moments that tried the souls of military daddies and mommies.

We had both had enough! Go find something to do, give us an hour, now go or else. That always meant I would put them to work cleaning, which was a fate worse than death to my kids. We finally got a few minutes of peace. Ron and I actually started making some good time and getting a lot done. Uh oh, when was the last time we heard the kids? We both said at the same time, "Go check on the kids." Both of us stopped right in the middle of doing something. Finally, Ron and I did what any mature mom and dad would do: paper, scissors, rock. I won, doing a fast winner dance and went right back to packing.

Two minutes after Ron left me, I heard something I very rarely ever heard Ron say. He swore. It was just the one word and nothing else, but that was just out of character for him. He seriously never did, so it had to be something big. As I was contemplating the actual swear, the next thing I heard were our blessed four children running for their lives and crying. Oh, for goodness sake, what could it be? I got up and ran up stairs to see kids flying in every direction and Ron with wet towels, face red, and pointing to our bed, the water bed. The kids thought they would help us by trying to empty the water bed on their own.

Not a good day in the Desautels' household on that particular afternoon, but it was kind of cute, in a very misguided way of course. To this very day, our grown children still talk about the day dad swore. Nice to know we left an impact on the kids. Of course we were hoping it would be over something besides Ron's swear word.

SCRIPTURE:

"Children, obey your parents in the Lord, for this is right.
"Honor your father and mother" which is the first commandment with the promise: that it may go well with you

and that you may live long in the land." Ephesians 6: 1-3 (NKJV)

DAY THREE HUNDRED FIFTY – "Something" is God's other name – "Something" told me to wait, "Something" told me to turn around, "Something" told me to give, "Something" woke me up to pray, and "Something" kept moving me forward. Whether you call Him "Something", God, Lord, El Shaddai, King, Yahwah, Father, Alpha and Omega, or the Great I AM. Know that He is in control, He is Sovereign, He is Holy, and He will take care of His own. He knows your name. He cares about the smallest details of your life, go to Him today and talk to Him. He has moved His entire schedule around just to hear from you.

DAY THREE HUNDRED FIFTY-ONE – Not forgiving is simply an act of pride – put pride aside and abide in the forgiveness of God's side.

DAY THREE HUNDRED FIFTY-TWO – How do you dress in the morning? Do you have a closet full of problems? Do you have one for each day of the week? Do you like to accessorize with hurt, self pity, anger and bitterness? I heard there was a big sale at the store, Judgment Hall, but some things, no matter how cheap should not be bought. I heard you purchased many of your items from the sales clerk, Enemy. Enemy doesn't care how you look; they just want the commission on the sale. My friend, it is time to clean out your closet. Next time you get dressed in the morning try putting on kindness, mercy, joy and grace. Accessorize with smile, patience, laughter and forgiveness.

DAY THREE HUNDRED FIFTY-THREE – You are not helpless. You have not lost control. You have not been defeated – as long as you continue to keep prayer first in your life. Push through, walk beside, head up, shoulders back – you can do this! Don't utter one word of defeat by complaining. Stand tall, be courageous; believe in who your prayers are going to. He will be your defense and your offense. You are not praying to thin air. Today could very well be the breakthrough you have been praying for. NEVER GIVE UP!

DAY THREE HUNDRED FIFTY-FOUR – Rise up. Spring forth. Roll over. Jump out of bed. Rejoice in the fact that He chose you first.

DAY THREE HUNDRED FIFTY-FIVE – Giving up and starting over are two separate choices. One will keep you sitting in the pew while the other one will let God know He has chosen well. Being still, or doing nothing, depends whose voice you listen to.

DAY THREE HUNDRED FIFTY-SIX – I love how the Bible shows me that God uses the common man, the flawed man, the last to be picked man to accomplish His will. That means there is hope for me and I am grateful for His touch on my life.

Message to my friends

I hope you know how unique you truly are to me. You are one of a kind, a gift from God to my life. I admire how you challenge yourself to go to the next level. I love your positive thoughts and actions. I love your laugh, your generous spirit, and you're not afraid to be silly. I love your humbleness and joy of life. I love how God knew that I needed you in this season of my life. I am humbled you pray for me, even when I was not very lovable. I love how you defend me even when I'm not around, you are my biggest cheerleader, and you inspire me to be a better person.

Sometimes I give more, but more often than not you are the one who does. We have been on some pretty amazing life journeys together, we have been poor together, we have gone on vacations together, we have prayed together, and we have even enjoyed alligator appetizers together. We are kindred spirits you and I, and I hope God sees fit to put us all in the same neighborhood in heaven together.

SCRIPTURE:

"This is my commandment that you love one another as I have loved you. Greater love has no one than this, than to lay down one's life for his friends. You are my friends if you do what I command you. No longer do I call you servants, for a servant does not know what his master is doing; but I have called you friends, for all that I have heard from my Father I have made known to you." John 15: 12-15 (NKJV)

DAY THREE HUNDRED FIFTY-SEVEN – I don't know about you, but I am encouraged when I hear about the struggles, the hurts, and even the pain of others. It brings their lives down to my level. Through Christ we can achieve anything. Greatness is born out of human failure, hardship, and heartache.

DAY THREE HUNDRED FIFTY-EIGHT – The middle of the night and early mornings are God's favorite times to speak to my spirit. I suppose I hear Him the best during these times because my soul is finally quiet and I am the most vulnerable. The Holy Spirit has opened my eyes to many truths during these times. Be encouraged, manifest hope, walk in faith, stay courageous, and stand strong – you were made for such a time as this!

DAY THREE HUNDRED FIFTY-NINE – Good morning Lord! You have greeted me with a breathtaking sunrise. You have shown me the complexity of what it takes to get the day moving. I stand in awe that you notice me. I marvel at your greatness, and humble myself before you. Let's start the day together!

DAY THREE HUNDRED SIXTY – I prayed to God that He would send someone to tell the lost about His grace and salvation. God answered – He was sending me.

DAY THREE HUNDRED SIXTY-ONE – Do you feel like you fail at everything you do? Do you feel frustrated, hurt, or lonely? Do you have broken relationships and you're not sure how to heal? Do you feel unlovable? Please listen to what I'm saying to you right now, "God loves you right where you are". Even if you have never gone to church, even if you have never prayed, even if you don't feel worthy – God wants me to tell you – Yes, you are His pride and joy. He wants you to come just as you are to Him. You don't have to do one extra thing to please Him, for His love for you is beyond our understanding. Let today be the day you start a new relationship with Him.

DAY THREE HUNDRED SIXTY-TWO – Forgiveness is the key to unlocking the favor of God.

DAY THREE HUNDRED SIXTY-THREE – Nothing is scarier and funnier than getting up in the middle of the night to go to the bathroom and having a shadow grab you. My eyes were half closed and arms outstretched so not to run in to any furniture, I suddenly sense a presence. I tell myself there is nothing to fear, there is nothing to fear, there is nothing to…and all of a sudden something grabs my arms. Not only did I scream bloody murder, but so did the shadowy figure in the night – It was Ron. Freakishly, he was going back to bed at the exact moment I was going in. On a side note: What is so funny about being scared? First we screamed, then there was nervous laughter, then we laughed harder, then we started to giggle, and then we fell asleep. A true senior moment.

DAY THREE HUNDRED SIXTY-FOUR – You can't live the glorious, favored life of God when everything out of your mouth is critical and bitter. Change the mind and the talk will follow. Change the heart and the glory will come. Increase your faith and watch God's grace move the mountain tops.

DAY THREE HUNDRED SIXTY-FIVE – "The Lord bless you and keep you; the Lord make his face shine upon you and be gracious to you; the Lord turn his face toward you and give you peace." Numbers 6:24-26 (NIV)

ACKNOWLEDGEMENT

When there are so many people in my life that have made such an impact, it is difficult to narrow it down to a mere sentence or to just a few people. I believe God has used people throughout my life to help mold me into the person I have become. There are also a few stand-outs, who during a crucial crossroad in my life, who actually took my hand and not only walked with me, but guided me, and some cases stood in front of me, protecting me.

Ron – For loving me unconditionally and bringing laughter and joy into our home. For always sharing the word of God in our home and for being the best husband, the best father, and truly one of the kindest men I have ever met in my life. On the night you proposed you said, "Marry me, and I'll treat you like a queen every day of your life" – and you have kept that promise.

My kids, Jessy, Jason, Josh, and Jenni - for letting me share parts of your life. Thank you for giving me so much to work with. God uses all things to glorify Him. You may not know this, but God knew exactly what kind of parents you would need. Unfortunately, they were all out at the time, so you got us. Remember God uses all things. Our family song - We are the Desautels', Mommy and Daddy Desautels, Jessica, Jason, Joshua, Jennifer Desautels. I love you, I treasure you, and yes, it is true, I do have a favorite one. I couldn't resist, just kidding. No, not really, I do. Just kidding once again, this never gets old.

Pat Moran – Mom, you have always set the example for us to follow. You have always been on our side. You continue to encourage us daily, and you are always looking at any situation with common sense and determination. Mom, you are the one who showed us if plan A doesn't work, that plans B thru Z can work out just as good, if not better. I love you.

Alexis Benander – You are my beloved friend and you have wanted me to write a book since we first met back in 1981. You prayed for me even when I wouldn't return the emails or phone calls. You sensed something was wrong. You have always understood me, which means you are either very holy or a little wicked. I love you both ways. You have always opened your home to us and Ron and I have always felt we are treasured guests.

Pam and Jeff Durham – Our life group leaders and our entire first life group – loving me right where I was; letting me share without judgment and letting me see your struggles too. You gave me the helping hand to get on with my spiritual journey.

Roxene Bacon – You loved me when I was a spiritual mess and you encouraged me to come to Life Group. Because of you, I am forever changed in my spiritual life. God ordained our friendship from the beginning.

Sara Marino – We met through your beautiful daughter, MaryAnn, and have stayed friends, showing that age does not matter. I love your strength in the face of much heartache. I love your enthusiasm for learning new things and for never giving up.

Craig Butler – I love your humble spirit. For your continual encouragement, and for your wicked sense of humor, and by wicked I really mean awesome. You may look like a kid to me, but your wisdom is like that of an old Godly man.

For my collage of eclectic Facebook friends – You all encouraged me to take the time to collect my thoughts and put them in book form. There was no mistake that our paths crossed in this moment in time. God used your voice, your words, and your prayers to lead me into the next part of my journey.

Tania Burgbacher – You were my mentor. You loved me where I was and you always spoke to me in love and truth. I know we are apart for a while, but when I get to heaven, I know we will have so much to share because of the words you gave me here on Earth.

For those who gave me special permission to tell their story, I will be forever grateful.

My Lord, My Father, My God –There is no possible way I could ever love you enough or serve you enough to equal your love for me. Even though you could have taken my life years ago, you saw some hope, some redemptive value, to use me once again to glorify your holy name. Above all these, I am most grateful for your Son, Jesus Christ. Because of Him, I can see tomorrow, I can have hope, love, and joy because He lives. My God, My Father, search my heart, for words alone can never express the love I have in my heart for you.

SPECIAL THANKS

Anthony Heyward – www.arhphoto.net – Thank you for having the patience to take many pictures of me, relaxed and at home. For capturing that ever important shot for the back cover.

Travis and Amy Schrock - maysevendesign.com - I appreciate the time you both took to make sure we shared the same vision and giving me a book cover that came to life.

Megan Burkheimer – Thank you for painstakingly editing my manuscript. You were very patient and accommodating for this nana.

Cindy Strickland and Jeanne Burgbacher – Thank you for taking time out of your busy schedules to read my manuscript before going to the publisher.

I would love to hear from you, please feel free to contact me through my email at snippetsnana@gmail.com. Share your testimony with me. How has God made a difference in your life?

If you would like to start a chapter of CLAP YOUR HANDS, in your area, please email me at claphands123@gmail.com and I will send you information on how we got started in the Low Country.

CPSIA information can be obtained
at www.ICGtesting.com
Printed in the USA
LVOW11s1506271116

514644LV00001B/81/P